Budget Beaters

Budget Beaters

Carmen Niehaus

Assisted by Lizbé Botha

Human & Rousseau

Cape Town • Johannesburg • Pretoria

Photographic credits

A special word of thanks to David Briers who photographed most of the dishes in this book.

I would also like to thank the following photographers:

Corrie Hansen: photographs on pp. 18 (bottom right), 22 (top right), 24 (top right), 25 (bottom left), 28 (bottom right), 49 (top right), 52 (bottom right), 58, 59 (top right), 65 (right), 75 (bottom left)

Ryno: photographs on pp. 10 (centre), 11 (right), 12 (right), 18 (top left), 41 (bottom right), 42 (left), 53 (top right), 69 (right)

Jacques Stander: photographs on pp. 8 (centre), 40 (top left), 66 (bottom left)

Cover photograph: Chicken and sweet potato potjie (p. 34)

Photographer: David Briers

Styling: Carmen Niehaus

First published in 1995 by Human & Rousseau (Pty) Ltd

State House, 3-9 Rose Street, Cape Town

English translation by Victor Lambert and Cecilia van Zyl

Illustrations by Piet Grobler

Typography and cover design by Etienne van Duyker

Styling by Carmen Niehaus

Text electronically prepared by Etienne van Duyker and Annelize van Rooyen

Colour reproduction by Hirt & Carter, Cape Town

Printed and bound by SNP Printing Pte Ltd, Singapore

ISBN 0 7981 3453 4

Contents

Nutritious fish 6

Tenderly stewed 14

Meals with mince and leftover meat 19

Dishes with sausages and bully beef 27

Liver and kidneys 31

Scrumptious chicken 34

Passion for pasta 38

Reliable rice dishes 45

Light meals 50

Bread as meals and snacks 56

Savoury vegetables 61

Puddings and sweets 71

Handy ready mixes 76

Index 79

Macaroni with pilchards in tomato sauce

Nutritious fish

Macaroni with pilchards in tomato sauce

Although pilchards in tomato sauce is her husband's favourite food, it wasn't necessarily hers, writes Cecilia Stapelberg of Krugersdorp West. But after reading how nutritious pilchards are – the bones, which are also edible, are packed with calcium – she decided to use pilchards instead of mince in their favourite macaroni dish.

1 packet (500 g) macaroni
2 cans (425 g each) pilchards in tomato sauce
1 large onion, finely chopped and sautéd in a little oil, if preferred
100 g (250 ml) Cheddar cheese, grated
3 extra-large eggs
250 ml milk
salt and pepper to taste
pinch cayenne pepper, if preferred
50 ml finely chopped parsley
1 tomato, sliced (optional)

Preheat the oven to 180 °C (350 °F). Spray a large ovenproof dish with non-stick spray.

Cook the macaroni in rapidly boiling salted water till done. Drain well. Spoon into the prepared dish. Flake the pilchards in the tomato sauce (reserve a few whole pilchards for garnishing) and mix with the onion. Spoon the mixture over the macaroni, add half the cheese and mix lightly.

Beat the eggs, milk and seasonings together and pour over the macaroni mixture. Arrange whole pilchards and tomato on top, season the tomato lightly with salt and pepper and sprinkle with the remaining cheese. Bake for about 30 minutes or till the egg mixture has set.

Serve with a salad.

Serves 8-10.

Fried pilchards

Fried pilchards

Her family is very fussy when it comes to food but they all love this quick and economic dish, writes Mrs Elize Steyn of Meerlus.

1 can (425 g) pilchards in tomato sauce
140 g (250 ml) cake flour
5 ml salt
black pepper to taste
2 eggs, whisked
oil for frying

Drain the pilchards and halve them. Do not remove the bones. Combine the cake flour, salt and black pepper and place on a plate.

Dip each pilchard half in the whisked eggs and then in the seasoned cake flour. Fry in enough heated oil till golden brown.

Serve with tartar sauce and a salad.

Serves 3-4.

Pilchards with yellow rice

The pilchards and vegetables are heated in a tasty sauce then spooned on top of yellow rice. Serve with a tomato and cucumber sambal, writes M Naicker of Halfway House.

500 ml rice
10 ml turmeric
salt
1 onion, sliced
5 ml crushed garlic
10 ml finely grated fresh ginger
1 green pepper, seeded and diced
oil
1 tomato, skinned and diced
1 large potato, peeled and diced
250 ml frozen peas
1 can (425 g) pilchards in chilli sauce

Boil the rice with the turmeric and salt in sufficient water till soft. Drain and keep warm.

Sauté the onion, garlic, ginger and green pepper in a little oil till soft. Add the tomato and diced potato and simmer till the potato is cooked. Add the peas and pilchards, including the sauce, and simmer till heated through. Spoon the rice onto a serving platter and spoon the fish mixture on top. Serve with a sambal of chopped tomato, cucumber, green chilli (optional) and a little lemon juice.

Serves 4.

Fish dish

Luiza van Vuuren of Valhalla makes a curried white sauce to which she adds a can of pilchards in tomato sauce.

1 large onion, finely chopped
30 ml margarine or butter
25 ml cake flour
250 ml milk
5-7 ml curry powder
5 ml salt
pinch pepper
1 can (425 g) pilchards in tomato sauce, slightly mashed
2 eggs, whisked

Preheat the oven to 180 °C (350 °F). Grease a 24-cm pie dish (or two smaller ones) with margarine.

Sauté the onion in the margarine or butter till soft. Remove from the heat and stir in the cake flour. Gradually stir in the milk, stirring till smooth. Heat once more while stirring continuously till the sauce comes to the boil and thickens. Add the seasonings and pilchards and heat till the sauce just comes to the boil. Cool slightly and stir in the whisked egg. Pour the mixture into the pie dish and bake for 45-60 minutes or till the mixture has set.

Serve with a salad.

Serves 4.

Pilchards with yellow rice

Fish dish

Pilchard pie

This was our first Budget Beater recipe, sent in by Mr Pieter Olivier of Parow, although the recipe for the crust is my Ouma Winnie's. If you like hot food use a can of pilchards in chilli sauce instead of a can of pilchards in tomato sauce.

Filling
2 onions, thinly sliced
1 green pepper, cut into strips
3 cloves garlic, crushed
oil
1 can (425 g) pilchards in chilli sauce, lightly flaked
1 can (425 g) pilchards in tomato sauce, lightly flaked
150 ml boiling water
30 ml lemon juice
5 ml basil
salt and pepper to taste
500 ml cooked pasta or rice

Crust
60 ml butter or margarine
90 ml cake flour
500 ml milk
salt and pepper to taste
2 eggs, whisked
5 ml baking powder

Preheat the oven to 190 °C (375 °F). Grease 1 large 26-cm dish or 3 smaller 16-cm dishes with margarine.

Sauté the onion, green pepper and garlic in a little oil till soft. Add both cans of pilchards and the boiling water. Heat till the sauce comes to the boil. Add the seasonings and the pasta or rice and mix lightly.

Spoon into the prepared dish.

Prepare the pastry: Melt the butter in a saucepan. Add the cake flour and stir to form a smooth paste. Remove from the heat and gradually stir in the milk. Heat, stirring continuously, till the sauce comes to the boil and thickens. Season with salt and pepper. Cool slightly and add the eggs, stirring continuously. Sift in the baking powder and mix well.

Pour over the pilchard mixture and bake till the crust is pale brown and puffed up.

Serves 6.

Hints
- For extra nourishment, add leftover vegetables to the filling and proceed as described.
- You can use the crust to make a pie from leftovers.

Haddock bake

Mrs Maureen Minty of Burgersdorp makes a delicious haddock dish with rice and a flavoursome cheese sauce.

1 packet (600 g) frozen haddock, defrosted
about 600 ml milk
50 ml butter or margarine
50 ml cake flour
5 ml mustard powder
salt
freshly ground black pepper
50 g (125 ml) Cheddar cheese, grated
1 onion, sliced
2 cloves garlic, crushed
little oil
50 ml finely chopped parsley
750 ml cooked rice

Preheat the oven to 180 °C (350 °F). Grease a medium ovenproof dish with margarine.

Skin the fish while still slightly frozen. Place the pieces of fish in a pan and pour over the milk. Simmer slowly till the fish is cooked and flakes easily with a fork. Drain, reserving the milk.

Melt the butter in the same pan, add the cake flour and stir to form a smooth paste. Heat, while stirring continuously, till the cake flour is cooked through. Add enough milk to the drained milk to make up 500 ml and slowly add to the cake flour paste.

Heat, stirring continuously till the white sauce comes to the boil and

Pilchard pie

Haddock bake

Haddock with sweetcorn

thickens. Season with the mustard powder and to taste with salt and black pepper. Add about half the Cheddar cheese, stirring till the cheese has melted.

Sauté the onion and garlic in a little oil till soft. Add the onion mixture and parsley to the cooked rice and mix well. Spoon into the prepared dish. Spoon the fish on top and pour over the white sauce.

Sprinkle with the remaining cheese and heat in the oven till the cheese has melted and the dish is heated through.

Serve with slices of lemon and a fresh salad, if preferred.

Serves 4-6.

Haddock with sweetcorn

Mrs Annatjie van den Berg of Discovery serves this dish with rice and a salad.

60 ml margarine
70 g (125 ml) cake flour
375 ml milk
7 ml salt
1 ml paprika
4 ml mustard powder
15 ml Worcester sauce
1 packet (600 g) haddock, cooked and flaked
1 can (410 g) cream-style sweetcorn
1 egg, lightly whisked
breadcrumbs for sprinkling on top
chopped parsley

Preheat the oven to 180 °C (350 °F). Grease an ovenproof dish with margarine.

Melt the 60 ml margarine and stir in the cake flour till a smooth paste is formed. Heat till the mixture comes to the boil. Stir continuously.

Slowly add the milk, stirring continuously. Heat till the mixture comes to the boil and thickens. Season, add the haddock, sweetcorn and whisked egg.

Turn the mixture into the prepared dish, sprinkle with breadcrumbs and bake for about 15-20 minutes or till the crumbs are browned.

Sprinkle with parsley.

Serves 4.

Haddock surprise

Here's another delicious haddock dish. Miss A Amsol of Lenasia uses shell noodles, but your favourite noodles will work just as well.

200 g shell noodles
600 g haddock
500 ml milk
1 onion, finely chopped
20 ml butter
40 ml cake flour

Haddock surprise

1 egg, beaten
100 g (250 ml) Cheddar cheese, grated
salt and pepper
1 ml cayenne pepper
juice and rind of 1 lemon
30 ml finely chopped parsley
fresh breadcrumbs

Preheat the oven to 180 °C (350 °F). Grease a medium ovenproof dish with margarine.

Boil the shell noodles in salted water till soft. Drain well.

Cook the haddock in the milk till done. Drain, reserving the milk. Flake the fish.

Sauté the onion in the butter till soft. Add the cake flour and stir for another minute. Remove from the heat and slowly add the reserved milk while stirring continuously.

Return the mixture to the stove and heat till the sauce comes to the boil and thickens. Stir continuously. Remove from the heat and add the egg, cheese and seasonings. Mix well. Add the haddock and mix lightly.

Spoon a layer of the haddock mixture into the prepared dish, then a layer of the shell noodles. Repeat the layers, ending with the haddock mixture.

Top with a sprinkling of fresh breadcrumbs and bake for 20 minutes or till the dish is heated through.

Serve with a salad.

Serves 6.

Malay haddock dish

Tuna macaroni

Tuna bake

Malay haddock dish

Mrs Susie Wilkenson of Grabouw often serves this dish for supper.

2 onions, sliced into rings
oil
2 large ripe tomatoes, skinned and finely chopped
4 x 250 ml cooked rice
3 pieces haddock
250 g frozen peas (optional)
salt and freshly ground black pepper to taste
1 or 2 hard-boiled eggs, shelled and sliced

Sauté the onion in a little oil till soft. Add the tomato and simmer till a purée is formed.

Mix the tomato and onion purée with the cooked rice and set aside.

Cook the haddock in a little water till done and till it flakes easily with a fork. Add to the rice mixture and mix lightly.

Boil the peas in a little water till done and mix with the rice mixture.

Season with salt and black pepper to taste. Spoon onto a serving platter. Slice the hard-boiled eggs and arrange on top.

Serve hot with a salad.

Serves 4.

Tuna macaroni

This filling dish is ideal for supper, writes Natalie Lourens of Rondebosch.

120 g (250 ml) elbow macaroni
1 can (200 g) tuna in brine, drained and flaked
50 ml butter or margarine
1 onion, finely chopped
50 ml cake flour
1 bay leaf
250 ml milk
salt and freshly ground black pepper
100 g (250 ml) grated Tusser's or Cheddar cheese
breadcrumbs for sprinkling on top

Preheat the oven to 180 °C (350 °F). Spray an ovenproof dish with non-stick spray.

Cook the macaroni in rapidly boiling salted water till just soft. Drain. Mix the macaroni with the tuna and spoon into the prepared dish.

Melt the butter and sauté the onion till soft. Add the cake flour and stir till a smooth paste is formed. Add the bay leaf and slowly add the milk, stirring continuously. Simmer till the sauce comes to the boil and thickens. Season with salt and black pepper to taste. Remove from the heat and stir in half the cheese. Pour the sauce over the macaroni mixture and sprinkle the remaining cheese and breadcrumbs on top. Heat about 20-30 minutes or till the cheese has melted and the dish is warmed through.

Serve immediately with a salad.

Serves 4.

Tuna bake

"Here's an old favourite from my recipe books. Served with a mixed salad, it makes a delicious Saturday evening supper for our family of four," writes Mrs Mariaan Odendaal of Virginia.

Mrs Odendaal sometimes sprinkles grated cheese on top. Alternatively, top with a sprinkling of fresh breadcrumbs.

1 onion, finely chopped
oil
1 can (200 g) tuna in brine
375 ml cooked rice
200 ml milk
100 ml mayonnaise
4 extra-large eggs
5 ml mustard powder
15 ml lemon juice
25 ml chopped parsley
salt
black pepper

Preheat the oven to 180 °C (350 °F). Grease a medium ovenproof dish with margarine.

Sauté the onion in a little heated oil till soft.

Drain and flake the tuna. Mix the onion, tuna and rice. Spoon into the prepared dish.

Beat the milk, mayonnaise and eggs together. Add the mustard powder, lemon juice and parsley. Season to taste with salt and black pepper and pour over the fish mixture in the dish. Bake for about 30 minutes or till the mixture has set and is golden brown on top.

Serves 4.

Tuna paella

She and her husband love seafood, writes Mrs Mari-Louise Guy of Observatory, but as they're both students they've had to devise this poor man's version of paella.

TUNA BALLS
1 can (200 g) tuna in brine, drained
1 medium-sized carrot, scraped and grated
1 slice bread, soaked in milk (squeeze out excess milk)
1 egg, whisked
salt and pepper to taste
oil for frying

RICE
1 onion, finely chopped
oil
10 ml turmeric
1 ml cayenne pepper
4 x 250 ml cooked rice
250 ml peas (optional)

Lightly mix all the ingredients for the tuna balls with a fork. Shape into balls and fry in a little oil till done. (Makes about 12 balls.) Keep warm.

Sauté the onion in a little heated oil till soft and add the turmeric and cayenne pepper. Add the rice and stir-fry till well mixed. Add the peas, if preferred, and heat till warmed through. Serve on a platter and arrange the tuna balls on top.

Serve with slices of lemon.

Serves 3-4.

Tuna pie

This tuna pie has a rice crust. Mrs Petro van der Watt of Port Elizabeth serves it with rolls and a salad.

500 ml cooked rice
15 ml grated onion
1 egg, whisked
1 can (200 g) tuna, drained
1 onion, coarsely chopped
100 g (250 ml) Cheddar cheese, grated
15 ml parsley, chopped
2 eggs
250 ml milk
3-5 ml Tabasco sauce
salt and pepper

Preheat the oven to 180 °C (350 °F). Grease a 23-cm pie dish with margarine.

Combine the cooked rice with the grated onion and whisked egg and line the pie dish with the mixture. Spoon the tuna on top and sprinkle with the chopped onion, grated Cheddar cheese and chopped parsley.

Whisk the eggs and milk together, season with Tabasco sauce and salt and pepper to taste and turn into the pie dish. Bake for about 45 minutes or till the filling has set.

Makes a medium-sized pie.

Tuna budget beater

Mrs Sheila Corrall of Uitenhage says she sometimes uses a can of bully beef instead of tuna to make this dish which also contains cabbage and carrot and is topped with a layer of mashed potato. We used tuna in oil and used the drained oil to fry the onion.

1-2 cans (200 g each) tuna in oil, drain, but reserve the oil
2 onions, finely chopped
2-3 cloves garlic, crushed
250 ml cabbage, finely shredded
pinch ground cumin (jeera) (optional)
4 fairly small carrots, scraped and cut into pieces
2 tomatoes, skinned and coarsely chopped
1 can (65 g) tomato paste
6 large potatoes, cooked and mashed

Preheat the oven to 180 °C (350 °F).

Heat the tuna oil and sauté the onion and garlic till soft. Add the finely shredded cabbage and cumin and stir-fry till the cabbage just turns glassy. Add the carrots, stir-fry for about 1 minute and add the tomatoes.

Reduce the heat and simmer till the carrots are just tender. Stir in the tomato paste as well as the tuna, add a little water if necessary and simmer for 1-2 minutes.

Turn the mixture into a fairly deep ovenproof dish, about 24 cm in diameter.

Pipe rosettes of mashed potato along the edges of the dish. Bake till the tips of the rosettes begin to brown.

Serve with a salad, if preferred.

Serves 4.

Tuna paella

Tuna pie

Tuna budget beater

Baked fish in mustard sauce

Hake with rice topping

Hake with tomato

Baked fish in mustard sauce

Mrs J G Rosser of Village of Happiness, Natal, bakes her fish in a tangy mustard sauce.

400 g fish fillets (about 4)
salt and pepper
10 ml prepared mustard
15 ml tomato purée
2 ml brown sugar
2 ml mixed herbs
60 ml cream

Preheat the oven to 180 °C (350 °F). Spray a medium ovenproof dish with non-stick spray.

Season both sides of the fish generously with salt and pepper and arrange the fillets in the prepared dish. Blend the remaining ingredients well and pour over the fish.

Bake for 20 minutes or till the fish is done and can be easily flaked with a fork.

Serve the flaked fish immediately with potatoes and a green salad.

Serves 4.

Hake with rice topping

Mrs Nikki Young of Brackenfell mixes rice with mayonnaise and vegetables like leeks and carrots and spoons the mixture on top of the fish.

Topping
3 leeks, well rinsed and sliced into thin rings
4 carrots, scraped and coarsely grated
about 75 ml butter or margarine
60 ml mayonnaise
250 ml cooked brown rice
50 g (125 ml) Cheddar cheese, grated (optional)
5 ml mixed dried herbs
pinch cayenne pepper

1 packet (600 g) frozen hake fillets, skinned and defrosted
salt and pepper to taste

Preheat the oven to 180 °C (350 °F). Grease an ovenproof dish with margarine.

Prepare the topping: Sauté the leeks and carrots in the butter till soft. Mix with the remaining ingredients for the topping and set aside.

Season the hake fillets to taste with salt and pepper and arrange in the prepared dish. Spoon the topping over the fish and bake for about 25 minutes or till the fish is done and flakes easily with a fork. Cover with tin foil if the topping becomes too dry. Serve with a mixed salad.

Serves 4.

Hake with tomato

Mrs Marie Potgieter of Humansdorp call this dish mnandi, which means “tasty”, in Zulu.

1 packet (750 g) hake
salt and freshly ground black pepper
juice of 1 lemon
1 onion, finely chopped
1 green or red pepper, seeded and finely chopped
oil
2 large ripe tomatoes, skinned and finely chopped
1 ml paprika
few drops Tabasco sauce
50 g (125 ml) grated Cheddar cheese
breadcrumbs for sprinkling on top

Preheat the oven to 200 °C (400 °F). Spray a medium ovenproof dish with non-stick spray.

Season the hake with salt and black pepper and lemon juice on both sides and arrange the fish in the prepared dish. Cover with tin foil and bake till the fish is done and can be easily flaked with a fork.

Sauté the onion and peppers in a little oil till soft. Add the tomatoes, paprika and Tabasco sauce and simmer till a fairly thick sauce is formed. Spoon over the cooked fish, sprinkle with cheese and breadcrumbs and return to the oven till the cheese has melted and the dish is warmed through.

Serve hot with rice, vegetables or a salad.

Serves 4.

Fish parcels

Nichola Southey of Steynsburg serves these fish parcels with potatoes baked in their jackets and a salad.

4-5 portions fish (any kind)
lemon juice
salt
180 ml mayonnaise
60-80 ml Dijon mustard
250 g button mushrooms, sliced

Preheat the oven to 200 °C (400 °F). Grease sheets of tin foil with margarine.

Sprinkle the fish with lemon juice and season lightly with salt. Place the fish on the sheets of tin foil. Blend the mayonnaise and mustard and spoon over each fish portion. Sprinkle with the mushrooms and spoon the remaining mayonnaise mixture on top. Close the tin foil parcels and bake for about 15 minutes or till it is easy to flake the fish with a fork. Open the tin foil parcels and bake for another 5 minutes.

Serves 4-5.

Fish curry

Serve this fish curry with yellow or white rice, pasta or mashed potato, writes Miss T B Haya of Bellville.

2-3 brinjals, cubed (optional)
salt
oil
1 onion, chopped
3 cloves garlic, crushed
30 ml curry powder
10 ml ground ginger
3 tomatoes, skinned and diced
600 g frozen fish fillets, cubed while still half-frozen
2 bay leaves
salt and black pepper to taste
3 spring onions, chopped (optional)

Sprinkle the cubed brinjal with salt and leave in a collander for about 15 minutes. Rinse under cold water and pat dry with paper towelling.

Heat a little oil in a pan and sauté the onion and garlic till soft. Add the brinjal cubes and stir till lightly browned. Add the curry powder and ginger and stir-fry for about 1 minute. Add the tomato and cubed fish and simmer till the fish flakes easily with a fork. Add the bay leaves and season to taste with salt and pepper. Sprinkle with chopped spring onions, if preferred.

Serves 4.

Curried fish pie

Mrs J van Tonder of Louis Trichardt was given this recipe by an old school friend, Marietjie, whose mother always made it for them during the school holidays. Add a can of curried vegetables if serving the pie as a main course.

CRUST
210 g (375 ml) cake flour
10 ml baking powder
2 ml salt
60 ml butter
1 extra-large egg, lightly beaten
15 ml oil
50-100 g (125-250 ml) Cheddar cheese, grated (optional)

FILLING
1 onion, finely chopped
1 tomato, skinned and finely chopped
1 can (410 g) curried vegetables
1 can (410 g) curried fish, flaked
3 extra-large eggs
60 ml milk
2 ml baking powder
salt
breadcrumbs for sprinkling on top

Preheat the oven to 180 °C (350 °F). Spray a deep ovenproof dish about 24 cm in diameter with non-stick spray.

Prepare the crust: Combine the cake flour, baking powder and salt. Rub the butter into the flour mixture till well blended. Add the egg and oil and mix. (The mixture will be fairly crumbly.) Press the mixture into the prepared ovenproof dish and chill. Sprinkle the crust with cheese, if preferred, before using the crust.

Mix the onion, tomato, curried vegetables and curried fish in a mixing bowl. Beat the eggs, milk and baking powder together and mix with the curried fish mixture. Season lightly with salt. Turn the mixture into the prepared crust and sprinkle with breadcrumbs. Bake for 30-45 minutes or till done and set.

Serve with a salad.

Serves 6.

Fish parcels

Fish curry

Curried fish pie

Shank casserole

Tenderly stewed

Shank casserole

Shin or shank is a relatively inexpensive cut of meat and can be used to make delicious dishes.

Katrien van Heerden of Forest Hill uses beef shin to make this dish, but mutton or pork shank can also be used. We used mutton shank to test the recipe.

2 onions, sliced
2 cloves garlic, crushed
1 green pepper, cut into strips
2 stalks celery, chopped
oil for frying
500 g cabbage, shredded
900 g mutton shank, cut into 2-cm thick pieces
salt and freshly ground black pepper
4 whole cloves
500 ml beef stock
1 bay leaf
large sprig fresh rosemary (optional)
20 ml white grape vinegar
100 g (125 ml) uncooked rice

In a large casserole, preferably a cast-iron pot, sauté the onion, garlic, green pepper and celery in oil till soft. Add the cabbage and stir-fry till tender but still crisp. Set aside.

Season the mutton shank with salt and black pepper to taste and fry, along with the cloves, till browned. Add more oil if necessary. Add the beef stock, the bay leaf, rosemary and vinegar. Reduce the heat and simmer till the meat is nearly done. Add the rice and simmer till the rice is done and most of the stock has been absorbed. (Add more stock or hot water if the dish becomes too dry.)

Return the vegetables to the casserole and heat through. Mix well and season with more salt and pepper if necessary.

Serve with sweet carrots, if preferred.

Serves 6-8.

Shank with delicious pie crust

Louisa Laubscher of Somerset West makes mutton shank in a thick gravy and tops it with this crust. But the crust is ideal to make a meal of any leftover meat.

1 onion, cut into pieces
oil
6 large pieces of mutton shank
cake flour seasoned with salt and pepper
meat stock, heated

CRUST
110 g (200 ml) cake flour
2 ml salt
6 ml baking powder
1 egg
125 ml buttermilk
125 ml oil

Preheat the oven to 180 °C (350 °F).

Sauté the onion in a little heated oil till soft. Roll the pieces of mutton shank in the seasoned cake flour and brown in heated oil. Add a generous amount of meat stock, reduce the heat, cover and simmer till the meat is tender. Add more meat stock, if necessary, and season with extra salt and pepper to taste. Turn the meat and sauce into an ovenproof dish.

Prepare the crust: Sift the dry ingredients together. Whisk the remaining ingredients together, mix with the dry ingredients and pour over the meat. Bake for about 25-30 minutes or till the crust is golden brown.

Serves 4.

Lamb shank in tin foil

Mrs Val Fraser of Durban North won the third prize in the Meat Board's Budget Beaters competition which were held in collaboration with *You*. The lamb shanks are served whole, making it easier to eat the last morsel of meat off the bone.

115 g (125 ml) butter or margarine
30 ml lemon juice
3 cloves garlic, crushed
10 ml dried or 30 ml fresh rosemary, chopped
10 ml dried or 30 ml fresh origanum, chopped
4 bay leaves
salt and freshly ground black pepper to taste
4 whole lamb shanks (about 600 g)
cornflour (optional)

Preheat the oven to 160 °C (325 °F) .

Melt the butter in a saucepan and add the remaining ingredients, except the lamb shanks and cornflour. Stir until the mixture starts to boil and remove from the heat.

Arrange all the pieces of meat on the shiny side of a sheet of tin foil and pour over the sauce mixture. Wrap the meat in the tin foil, sealing it so that the steam cannot escape. Place the parcel in an ovenproof dish and bake for about 2 hours or till the meat is tender.

Thicken the sauce with a little cornflour, if necessary, and serve with the shanks.

Serves 4.

Shank with delicious pie crust

Lamb shank in tin foil

Canned potjie

Canned potjie

Mrs R Keet of Westonaria uses canned vegetables like whole kernel sweetcorn, green beans and peas to make a delicious potjie. Cook the meat and potatoes in the reserved vegetable liquid.

1-4 pieces shoulder bacon
1 large onion, sliced into rings
2 cloves garlic, crushed
oil
6 neck of mutton slices, each 2 cm thick
salt and freshly ground black pepper
3 large ripe tomatoes, skinned and finely chopped
6 potatoes, peeled and quartered
1 can (420 g) whole kernel sweetcorn, drained, but liquid reserved
1 can (410 g) green beans, drained, but liquid reserved
1 can (410 g) peas, drained, but liquid reserved
6 potatoes, peeled and quartered
little basil or origanum

Fry the bacon till done. Add the onion and garlic and sauté till soft. Add a little oil if necessary.

Using a sharp knife, score the fatty sides of the mutton neck slices. Season to taste with salt and black pepper, add to the onion mixture and fry till brown. Add the tomato and drained vegetable liquid (which has been slightly heated) and simmer till the meat is just tender. Add the potatoes and simmer till the meat is tender and the potatoes are soft. Add more liquid, if necessary. Add the canned vegetables and simmer till heated through. Season with basil or origanum and with extra salt and pepper, if preferred.

Serve with rice.

Serves 6.

Shank with beans and samp

Her mother often made this dish when she had many mouths to feed, writes Mrs Cathy Immelman of Framesby, Port Elizabeth. The dish is not only economical but also very tasty.

Bean mixture

6 pieces shank
salt and freshly ground black pepper
oil
1 large onion, sliced
1 green pepper, cut into strips
10 ml curry powder
5 ml ground cumin (jeera)
5 ml ground coriander
5 ml ground ginger
2 large tomatoes, skinned and chopped
250-500 ml hot water
cake flour
500-750 ml cooked kidney beans

Samp

500 ml samp, soaked overnight in cold water
salt
150 ml milk (optional)
15-30 ml butter or margarine
pinch sugar
chopped parsley

Season the meat well with salt and black pepper. Brown in a little heated oil. Remove from the pan.

Sauté the onion and green pepper in the oil in the pan till soft. Add the curry powder, cumin, coriander and ginger and stir-fry for about 1 minute. Add the tomatoes and simmer till soft. Add the shank and 250-500 ml hot water and simmer till the meat is tender. There should be a generous amount of gravy. Thicken the gravy with a little cake flour blended with a little water. Add the kidney beans and mix. Heat till warmed through and season with extra salt and pepper if necessary.

Drain the samp and cover with fresh cold water. Boil till the samp is soft. Season well with salt. Add milk, butter and a pinch of sugar. Mash slightly with a potato masher. Heat till warmed through, taking care that the samp does not stick to the bottom of the pan.

Spoon onto a serving dish. Serve the beans with the samp and sprinkle with parsley.

Serves 6.

Shank with beans and samp

Hearty beef stew

Hearty beef stew

Filling and nourishing and perfect for supper on a cold winter's evening. Mrs C Swart of Mossel Bay says this is one of her favourite recipes.

1,2 kg deboned stewing beef, cut into strips
salt
freshly ground black pepper
about 110 g (200 ml) cake flour
oil
10 whole pickling onions, skinned
1 can (410 g) tomato purée
15-20 ml mustard powder
5 ml dried rosemary or 1 sprig fresh rosemary
250-500 ml hot water
4 large potatoes, peeled and quartered

Season the strips of beef well with salt and black pepper. Roll in the cake flour and brown small quantities of the meat at a time in heated oil. Add the onions and stir-fry till glossy. Add the tomato purée and mustard powder, mix well and season with the rosemary. Add half the hot water, reduce the heat, cover and simmer till the meat is nearly tender. Add the potatoes and more hot water if necessary and simmer till the meat is tender and the potatoes are soft and cooked. The gravy should be thick and flavoursome. Season with more salt and pepper if necessary.

Serve with rice and vegetables.

Serves 8.

HINTS:

- Suitable cuts of meat for this dish are: bolo, hump, thick flank, topside and aitchbone.
- You can also use sheep shank or neck.

Beef shin casserole

Mrs Luiza van Vuuren of Valhalla, Pretoria, makes a tasty casserole with beef shin and potatoes and uses a packet of mushroom soup powder to make the sauce.

4-6 pieces beef shins, each about 1,5 cm thick
salt and pepper
1 onion, coarsely chopped
oil
hot water
few springs fresh rosemary
1 bay leaf
4 potatoes, skinned and coarsely chopped
2 tomatoes, skinned and coarsely chopped
half a 61-g packet mushroom soup powder

Lightly season the shins with salt and pepper and fry with the onion in a little oil till the meat has browned on the outside. Add a little hot water and simmer till the meat is nearly tender. Season with a few sprigs fresh rosemary and a bay leaf. Add the potatoes and simmer till soft, adding more water as needed. Transfer the potatoes and meat to a serving dish. Keep warm.

Add the tomatoes to the meat sauce in the saucepan and simmer till the tomatoes form a purée. Stir in the mushroom soup powder and more hot water and heat till the sauce comes to the boil and thickens slightly. Pour over the meat and potatoes and serve with rice.

Serves 4-6.

Beef shin casserole

Beer stew

Beer stew

The beer gives the meat an interesting flavour, but take care that you do not add too much otherwise the flavour is overpowering. Florence Mbatha of Kwa-Thema, Springs serves the stew with mealie meal porridge or mashed potato.

1 kg beef shin, cut into 1,5-cm pieces
salt and black pepper to taste
oil
1 onion, sliced
2 cloves garlic, crushed
250 ml beer
beef stock, made with a stock cube and 500 ml boiling water
4 potatoes, peeled and cut into pieces
5 ml mixed herbs
chopped parsley

Using a sharp knife, score the sides of the meat to prevent it from curling while cooking. Season the meat to taste with salt and black pepper.

Heat a little oil in a flat-bottomed cast-iron pot and fry the meat till lightly browned on both sides. Remove from the pot and sauté the onion and garlic in the oil in the pot till soft. Return the meat to the pot. Blend the beer with the heated beef stock and add a little of the mixture to the meat. Cover the pot, reduce the heat and simmer till the meat is nearly tender.

Add the potatoes when the meat is almost tender. Add more beer and meat stock as the pot boils dry. Simmer till the meat and potatoes are done. Season with extra salt and pepper if necessary and with the mixed herbs. Sprinkle with chopped parsley just before serving.

Serves 4.

Beef stew

Hester Coetzee of Hopefield was given this recipe by a friend, Joyce Sauer. She usually places the dish in the oven in the morning before leaving for work and by the time she arrives home it is deliciously tender and flavoursome (see variation). We prepared the stew on the stove top.

1 large onion, sliced
2-3 cloves garlic, crushed
1 green pepper, diced
oil
1 kg stewing beef, cubed
black pepper to taste
about 12,5 ml soy sauce
140 g (250 ml) cake flour
1 ml ground cloves
2 ml nutmeg
half a 71-g packet white onion soup powder
625 ml water
125 ml milk
salt

Sauté the onion, garlic and green pepper in a little heated oil till soft. Remove from the pan and set aside.

Season the beef cubes to taste with black pepper and sprinkle with soy sauce. Combine the cake flour, ground cloves and nutmeg. Roll the beef cubes in the mixture and brown small quantities of the meat at a time in heated oil. Drain most of the oil, and return the onion mixture to the pan.

Blend the soup powder with the water and add the milk. Pour the mixture over the beef cubes. Heat, stirring continuously, till the sauce comes to boil. Reduce the heat, cover partially and simmer till the meat is tender and the gravy has thickened. Season with extra salt and pepper, if necessary.

Serve with samp and sweet carrots or peas.

Serves 6.

VARIATION

• Follow the method as described till the sauce starts to boil. Spoon the meat mixture into an ovenproof dish, cover, and bake slowly at 100 °C (200 °F) till the meat is tender and done.

Beef stew

Mince pie with crumb topping

Meals with mince and leftover meat

MINCE

Mince pie with crumb topping

Make mince go further by adding a can of baked beans in tomato sauce, writes Mrs Anna-Marie Venter of Duiwelskloof. The crumb topping is delicious with the mince and makes the dish very filling.

1 onion, finely chopped
2 cloves garlic, crushed
oil
500 g mince
1 can (410 g) baked beans in tomato sauce
15 ml Worcester sauce
few drops Tabasco sauce
salt and black pepper

50 g (60 ml) butter
100 g (200 ml) cake flour
2 ml basil
15 g (200 ml) Cheddar cheese, grated

Preheat the oven to 180 °C (350 °F). Grease an ovenproof dish with margarine.

Sauté the onion and garlic in a little oil in a pan till soft. Add small quantities of the mince at a time, and brown lightly. Add the baked beans and season with the Worcester sauce, Tabasco sauce and salt and black pepper to taste. Spoon into the prepared dish.

Rub the butter into the cake flour using your fingertips till the mixture resembles breadcrumbs. Add the basil and Cheddar cheese and mix well. Sprinkle over the mince mixture and bake for about 20-30 minutes till the topping is golden brown.

Serve with a salad.

Serves 4-6.

Curry bake

Since Ria van Tonder of Strubenvale, Springs, served this curried mince dish from one of the cookery books she has compiled herself, it has become a family favourite.

CURRIED MINCE
1 large onion, sliced
2 cloves garlic, crushed
oil
25 ml mild curry powder
5 ml ground ginger
2 ml ground coriander
pinch nutmeg
50 ml brown vinegar
500 g mince
1 can (410 g) whole, peeled tomatoes, finely chopped
2 bay leaves
60 ml brown or white sugar
salt and freshly ground black pepper to taste

CRUST
300 g (625 ml) cake flour
15 ml baking powder
3 ml salt
25 ml mild curry powder
100 g butter or margarine, grated
1 large onion, grated
2 cloves garlic, crushed
2 eggs, lightly whisked
cold water

Dumplings and curried mince

Preheat the oven to 180 °C (350 °F).

Prepare the mince: Sauté the onion and garlic in a little oil till soft. Add the curry, ginger, coriander and nutmeg and stir-fry for about 1 minute. Add the vinegar and simmer for 1 minute. Add small quantities of the mince at a time and fry till done. Add the tomatoes, bay leaves and sugar and simmer till the mixture thickens. Season well with salt and pepper. Spoon into an ovenproof dish.

Prepare the crust: Sift the dry ingredients together. Rub in the butter with your fingertips till the mixture resembles breadcrumbs.

Add the onion and garlic and mix. Add the beaten eggs and mix lightly to form a stiff dough. (Add a little cold water if necessary.) On a floured surface, roll the dough about 2 cm thick and cut out circles with a cookie cutter. Cover the mince with the circles. Bake for 30-35 minutes or till the crust is light brown and done.

Serve with rice and chutney, banana slices, coconut and finely chopped tomato and onion sambal.

Serves 6-8.

Curry bake

Dumplings and curried mince

Mabel Leshaba of Mamelodi West makes mealie meal dumplings which she serves on curried mince.

CURRIED MINCE
1 onion, sliced
2 cloves garlic, crushed
oil
15 ml curry powder
10 ml turmeric
750 g lean mince
250 ml meat stock, heated
15 ml tomato paste
15 ml white sugar
15 ml Worcester sauce
salt and pepper to taste
15 ml cake flour

DUMPLINGS
70 g (125 ml) mealie meal
70 g (125 ml) cake flour
10 ml baking powder
3 ml salt
150 ml water

Samp bobotie (1)

Samp bobotie (2)

Sauté the onion and garlic in a little heated oil till soft. Add the curry powder and turmeric and stir-fry for about 1 minute. Add the mince and fry till done. Mix the meat stock with the tomato paste, sugar and Worcester sauce and add to the mince mixture. Season to taste with salt and pepper, sprinkle with cake flour and simmer till the meat is done and the sauce has thickened slightly.

Mix all the ingredients for the dumplings together and drop spoonfuls on top of the mince. Cover and simmer for about 10 minutes or till the dumplings are done.

Serve with chutney and a salad.

Serves 4-6.

Samp bobotie (1)

Add samp to this tasty bobotie recipe to make it go further. Connie Blignaut of Port Elizabeth serves the bobotie with chutney and a salad.

500 ml samp, soaked overnight
10 ml turmeric
salt
2 large onions, sliced
oil for frying
25 ml hot curry powder
1 kg mince
50 ml chutney
30 ml sugar
10 ml tomato paste
60 ml grape vinegar
salt and pepper
250 ml milk
2 eggs
2 bay leaves

Preheat the oven to 180 °C (350 °F). Spray a large ovenproof dish with non-stick spray.

Drain the samp and cover with fresh cold water. Add about 5 ml turmeric to the water and boil the samp till soft and cooked. Season to taste with salt towards the end of the cooking time. Drain and set aside.

Sauté the onions in a little heated oil till soft. Add the curry powder and the rest of the turmeric and stir-fry for about 1 minute. Add small quantities of the mince at a time and fry till done. Add the remaining seasonings and season to taste with salt and pepper. Simmer for another few minutes. Add the samp and mix. Turn into the prepared dish.

Beat the milk and eggs together and pour over the mince mixture. Place the bay leaves on top and bake for 30-40 minutes or till the egg mixture has set and is pale brown.

Serves 10.

Samp bobotie (2)

Similar to the previous bobotie recipe, but with different seasonings. Mrs Bettie van Tonder of Monte Vista sprinkles cheese over the dish, but we think it's just as good without.

375 ml uncooked samp, soaked overnight
salt
little butter or margarine
milk (optional)
Cheddar cheese, grated (optional)
500 g mince
oil
5 ml curry powder
2 ml ground cumin (jeera)
100 ml tomato sauce
100 ml chutney
pinch nutmeg
black pepper to taste
100 ml raisins (optional)
2 eggs
250 ml milk

Preheat the oven to 180 °C (350 °F). Grease an ovenproof dish with margarine.

Drain the samp and cover with fresh cold water. Boil till soft and season with salt only at the end of the cooking time. Drain and mash lightly. Add a knob of butter or margarine and a little milk, if preferred. Spoon the samp into the bottom of the ovenproof dish and spread evenly. Grate a little Cheddar cheese on top, if preferred.

Fry small quantities of the mince at a time in a little heated oil. Add the curry powder and cumin and fry until the mince is done. Blend the tomato sauce and chutney and add. Season to taste with salt, nutmeg and black pepper. Add the raisins if preferred. Spoon the mince mixture on top of the cheese and spread evenly.

Beat the eggs and milk together, season to taste with salt and pepper and pour over the mince mixture. Bake till the egg mixture has set, about 30-40 minutes.

Serve with a salad, if preferred.

Serves 6.

Mealie meal and mince casserole

Easy to make and very satisfying, writes Mrs Nicoleen Kriek of Vredefort.

140 g (250 ml) mealie meal
500 ml water
5 ml salt
1 onion, coarsely chopped
½ green pepper, diced
15 ml oil
500 g mince
pinch braai spice
salt and pepper to taste
60 ml tomato sauce
1 tomato, sliced
2 eggs
125 ml milk

Preheat the oven to 180 °C (350 °F). Grease an ovenproof dish with margarine.

Blend the mealie meal, water and salt together in a saucepan and boil till the porridge is cooked. Stir occasionally.

Sauté the onion and green pepper in the heated oil till soft. Add the mince and fry till done, but not browned. Season with the braai spice and salt and pepper to taste. Add the tomato sauce and mix. Mix the mince with the porridge and spoon into a prepared dish. Place the tomato slices on top and season lightly with salt and pepper.

Beat the eggs and milk together and pour on top. Bake for about 30 minutes or till the egg mixture has set.

Serve with a salad.

Serves 4-6.

Putu with mince

Putu pap is a real treat in their home, writes Hannatjie Pienaar of George.

Putu pap
500 ml boiling water
salt
180 g (375 ml) mealie meal

Mealie meal and mince casserole

Putu with mince

Mince
1 onion, sliced
oil
500 g mince
2 tomatoes, skinned and coarsely chopped
250 ml chicken stock
75 ml tomato purée or 1 can (65 g) tomato paste
little sugar
salt and black pepper to taste

Pour the boiling water into a saucepan. Add about 3 ml salt. Add all the mealie meal at once so that it lies in a heap in the centre of the saucepan. Do not stir. Cover and heat slowly for about 10-15 minutes or till a thin layer has formed over the mealie meal. Stir the mixture with a fork till it is loose and crumbly. Cover and heat for about 15-30 minutes more till the pap is dry and crumbly. Stir once more to crumble.

In the meantime prepare the mince: Sauté the onion in a little oil till soft. Add small quantities of the mince at a time and fry till brown. Stir with a fork. Add the tomatoes. Blend the chicken stock with the tomato purée and add to the mince mixture. Reduce the heat and simmer till the tomatoes have formed a purée and the mince has formed a generous gravy. Season with a little sugar and salt and black pepper.

Serve the mince with the putu pap.

Serves 4.

Savoury mince and rice

You can prepare the rice and mince separately or in one pot as suggested by Miss E Visser of Wierdapark, Verwoerdburg (see variation on p. 23).

200 g (250 ml) rice
750 ml chicken stock

Mince mixture
1 onion, sliced
2 cloves garlic, crushed
½ green pepper, diced
½ red pepper, diced
2 stalks celery, cut into 1-cm pieces
3 medium-sized carrots, cleaned and cut into 1-cm pieces
oil

750 g mince
1 can (65 g) tomato paste
125 ml chicken stock
ground coriander
nutmeg
salt and black pepper

Rinse the rice well. Pour over the chicken stock and boil the rice till soft and done. Replenish the liquid with water, if necessary.

In the meantime, prepare the mince mixture: Sauté the onion, garlic, peppers and celery in a little oil till soft and glossy. Add the carrot and stir-fry till glossy. Remove from the pan and set aside.

Brown small quantities of the mince at a time in the oil in the pan. Blend the tomato paste and chicken stock and pour over. Season to taste with coriander and nutmeg as well as a little salt and black pepper, if necessary. Add the sautéed vegetables, cover and simmer till the carrots are just soft and most of the stock has evaporated but the mixture is not dry.

Spoon the rice on a serving platter and spoon the mince mixture on top.

Serve with a salad, if preferred.

Serves 6.

VARIATION

• You can also prepare the dish in one pot: Prepare the mince as described, season, add the vegetables, but do not simmer the mixture. Add the uncooked rice, as well as the 750 ml chicken stock and simmer till most of the liquid is absorbed and till the rice is tender and cooked.

Instant supper

Mrs Sarie Koen of Dawn View says if unexpected guests drop by and you want to chat instead of slaving over a hot stove in the kitchen, try this dish which is quick and economical.

Savoury mince and rice

Instant supper

6 slices bread, each about 2 cm thick, crusts removed
oil
3 onions, chopped
1 clove garlic, crushed
3 ml curry powder
250 g mince
3 tomatoes, skinned and coarsely chopped
15 ml lemon juice
salt and pepper to taste

Using a cookie cutter, cut a 5-cm circle from each slice of bread and fry in a little oil till golden brown. Alternatively, toast the bread under the oven grill.

Sauté the onion and garlic in a little oil till soft. Add the curry powder and stir-fry for about 1 minute. Add the mince and fry till done. Add the tomato and simmer till soft. Season with lemon juice and salt and pepper to taste.

Place the slices of bread on a plate and top each with a little of the mince mixture.

Serve with a salad.

Serves 4-6.

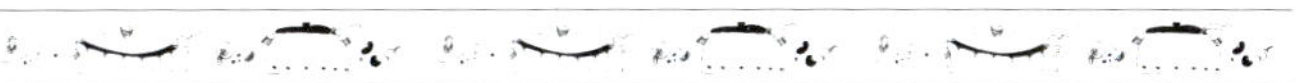

TOPPINGS FOR STEWS, MINCE OR LEFTOVER MEAT

• Transform a stew into a pie by covering it with scone or pie dough; bake at 200 °C (400 °F) till golden brown.
• Spoon mashed potatoes on top of a stew, brush with whisked egg and bake at 200 °C (400 °F).
• Prepare a vegetable crust by making a thick white sauce and folding leftover vegetables into the mixture. Pour over the meat and bake at 200 °C (400 °F) till golden brown.
• Sprinkle a mixture of fresh breadcrumbs and Cheddar or Parmesan cheese over the dish and grill it.
• Roll frozen pastry out till thin, spread with a flavoured butter like parsley or garlic butter and roll it up. Cut into wheels, arrange on top of meat and bake in a preheated oven at 200 °C (400 °F) till golden brown.
• Mix 250 ml plain yoghurt, 2 eggs, 5 ml prepared mustard, salt, pepper and 50 g (125 ml) grated Cheddar cheese. Spoon the mixture on top of the meat and bake for 45 minutes at 160 °C (325 °F).

Mince surprise

Mrs N Stadler of Noorder-Paarl came second in the Meat Board's Budget Beaters competition.

MINCE
1 kg beef mince
30 ml cooking oil
1 onion, chopped
250 ml tomato sauce
salt and freshly ground black pepper to taste

SALAD DRESSING
500 ml natural yoghurt
30 ml fresh parsley, chopped
30 ml grape vinegar

SALAD
1 medium-sized head of lettuce, shredded or broken into small pieces
½ English cucumber, diced
2 tomatoes, diced or 4-6 cherry tomatoes, halved
4-6 carrots, coarsely grated or cut into strips with a vegetable parer
6-8 packets tomato-flavoured Fritos

Fry small quantities of the mince at a time in a little heated oil till the meat just begins to turn colour. Stir continuously with a fork. Remove the mince to a side dish.

Sauté the onion in the same saucepan till soft. Return the meat to the saucepan and add the tomato sauce. Season to taste with salt and pepper. Cover and simmer slowly for 20-30 minutes till the mince forms a flavoursome sauce and is heated through. Turn the mince mixture into a serving bowl. Keep warm.

In the meantime, prepare the salad dressing: Blend all the ingredients for the salad dressing and spoon into a bowl.

Arrange the shredded lettuce in a bowl and arrange the remaining salad ingredients on top. Mix lightly with a salad spoon and fork.

Place the Fritos in a bowl. Serve the ingredients separately so that each person can assemble his or her own meal as follows (alternatively, assemble the ingredients on each plate beforehand): Place a layer of Fritos on the plate and spoon a layer of mince on top, followed by a generous helping of salad. Moisten with the salad dressing.

Serves 6-8.

Mince surprise

Mince meat loaf

Mince meat loaf

Make mince go further by adding mashed beans. Mrs J de Maroussem of Camperdown sent us the recipe.

180 g (250 ml) uncooked sugar beans, soaked in water and boiled
1 onion, finely chopped
2 cloves garlic, crushed
oil
450 g mince
pinch cayenne pepper
salt and freshly ground black pepper to taste
2 ml ground coriander
75 ml of the water in which the sugar beans were cooked
50 ml tomato sauce or paste
5 ml chutney
5 ml Marmite
500 ml boiled rice
100 ml finely chopped parsley
40 g (100 ml) Cheddar cheese, finely grated (optional)
1 small tomato, sliced (optional)

Preheat the oven to 180 °C (350 °F). Grease a 23 x 13 x 7-cm loaf tin with margarine.

Drain the cooked beans, reserving the water. Mash the beans.

Sauté the onion and garlic in a little oil till soft. Cool and add to the uncooked mince. Add the mashed beans. Season with the cayenne pepper, salt and black pepper to taste and the coriander. Blend 75 ml of the bean water with the tomato sauce, chutney and Marmite. Mix well. Add to the meat mixture. Divide the mixture in 3.

Mix the rice, parsley and Cheddar cheese. Divide in half.

Arrange the tomato slices on the base of the prepared loaf tin. Spread one-third of the meat mixture evenly on top. Add one half of the rice mixture and spread evenly. Repeat the layers, ending with a layer of the mince mixture. Press into the tin and bake for 40-60 minutes or till cooked through.

Serve warm.

Serves 4-6.

MEATBALLS

Meatballs and beans

These meatballs are made with boerewors but you can use ordinary mince if you prefer. The sauce makes this a delicious and very filling meal. Mrs S M du Preez of Swartruggens enjoys making this dish.

MEATBALLS
2-3 slices white bread, crusts removed
100 ml chicken stock
400 g boerewors or 400 g mince
1 onion, chopped
salt and freshly ground black pepper to taste
25-30 ml chopped parsley
oil

SAUCE
1 can (410 g) whole tomatoes, chopped
125 ml white wine
15 ml sugar
5 ml paprika
pinch nutmeg
125 ml cream
500 ml cooked kidney beans

Soak the bread in the chicken stock. Remove the sausage meat from the casings and mix with the soaked bread and the chopped onion. Season with salt and black pepper and parsley. Shape the mixture into about 24 small or 12 fairly large meatballs. Fry till brown on the outside and cooked inside. Remove from the pan and set aside.

Pour the tomatoes and white wine into the pan and boil till the tomatoes have formed a purée and most of the liquid has evaporated. Season with sugar, paprika and a pinch of nutmeg. Add the cream and simmer till the sauce is nice and thick. Add the kidney beans, mix and season with salt and pepper if necessary. Arrange the meatballs on top, cover and heat slowly till the dish is warmed through. Stir to prevent the mixture from sticking to the bottom of the pan.

Serves 6.

Meatballs and beans

Meatballs with apple sauce

Meatballs with apple sauce

The apple sauce goes very well with the meatballs. Mrs Dottie Luus of Secunda says this dish often saves the day when unexpected guests arrive at dinner time.

MEATBALLS
500 g mince
2 thick slices brown bread (crusts removed), soaked in water till soft
1 onion, finely chopped
1 ml nutmeg
1 ml ground ginger
salt and pepper to taste
1 egg, beaten
oil for frying

SAUCE
1 onion, sliced
2 cloves garlic, crushed
2-3 apples, skinned and diced
15 ml soy sauce
300 ml chicken stock or water
10 ml fresh sage, finely chopped
2 ml ground ginger
10 ml sugar
cornflour

Mix all the ingredients for the meatballs in a large mixing bowl. Shape into meatballs and fry in oil till browned on the outside and cooked inside. Remove from the pan. Keep warm.

Sauté the onion and garlic in the same pan till soft. Add the diced apple and stir-fry for about 5 minutes till transparent.

Add the soy sauce and chicken stock and bring to the boil. Add the remaining ingredients, except the cornflour. Simmer till the diced apple is soft.

If necessary, thicken the sauce with cornflour which has been blended with a little water. Simmer till the sauce thickens.

Pour the sauce over the meatballs and serve the dish immediately.

Serves 6.

VARIATION
• Fry the meatballs in oil till brown on the outside, spoon into an ovenproof dish and pour the sauce over. Cover and bake for about 20 minutes in a moderate oven at 160 °C (325 °F) till the meatballs are cooked and have absorbed some of the sauce.

LEFTOVER MEAT

Leftover meat with Cheddar crumb crust

First-prize winner in the Meat Board's Budget Beaters competition which were held in collaboration with *You,* was Mrs D Thuysse of Malmesbury. She makes a tasty dish with lamb coated with sauce and covered with a cheese crumb crust.

500 g cooked leftover lamb, cubed
1 onion, coarsely chopped
80 g (175 ml) cake flour
15 ml tomato purée
250 ml meat stock
5 ml salt
freshly ground black pepper to taste

CRUMB CRUST
50 ml butter
100 g (250 ml) Cheddar cheese, grated
3 ml mixed spice

Preheat the oven to 160 °C (325 °F).

Mix the cubed lamb and chopped onion. Blend 15-30 ml of the cake flour, the tomato purée and meat stock and pour over the meat mixture. Season with salt and black pepper to taste and turn the mixture into an ovenproof dish.

Rub the butter with your fingertips into the remaining cake flour till the mixture resembles breadcrumbs. Add the Cheddar cheese and mixed spice, mixing well. Spoon over the meat mixture in the dish and bake for about 45 minutes till the crumb crust is straw-coloured and the meat mixture heated through.

Serve with a salad.

Serves 4-6.

Leftover meat rolled in scone dough

Use any leftover stewed meat and wrap it in your favourite scone dough. Mrs Julie van Niekerk of Bushmans River Mouth, sent us this idea. Here is our recipe for leftover meat along with our favourite scone recipe.

Leftover meat with Cheddar crumb crust

Leftover meat rolled scone dough

MINCE
1 onion, sliced
2 cloves garlic, crushed
oil for frying
500 g mince
4 ml salt
freshly ground black pepper to taste
3 ml basil
6 ml sugar
1 can (410 g) tomatoes, chopped
250 ml cooked rice
180 ml All Bran flakes (optional)

SCONE DOUGH
240 g (500 ml) cake flour
12,5 ml baking powder
2 ml salt
90 g (100 ml) margarine
1 egg
125 ml milk

Preheat the oven to 180 °C (350 °F). Spray a baking sheet with non-stick spray.

Sauté the onion and garlic in a little heated oil till soft. Brown small quantities of the mince at a time till cooked.

Add the seasonings and tomatoes. Reduce the heat and simmer till the sauce has thickened.

Remove from the heat and cool. Add the rice and All Bran flakes and mix well.

Sift the dry ingredients together in a mixing bowl. Rub in the margarine with your fingertips till the mixture resembles breadcrumbs.

Whisk the egg and milk and add just enough of the liquid to the dry ingredients to form a soft dough which can easily be rolled. Mix with a spatula till just blended.

On a floured surface, roll the dough into a 2-cm thick rectangle. Spoon the mince mixture on top and carefully roll up the dough lengthwise. Place on the prepared baking sheet and bake for 20 minutes or till the dough is cooked through and golden brown. Cover with tin foil if the dough becomes too dark.

Slice and serve with a green salad.

Serves 6.

Pap and wors

Dishes with sausages and bully beef

Pap and wors

Make a mielie pap and boerewors pie and serve with a chilli tomato sauce, writes Mrs Nikki Young of Brackenfell.

600 g boerewors
120 g (250 ml) mealie meal
625 ml water
salt
80 g (200 ml) Cheddar cheese, grated
1 can (410 g) tomato and onion mix
25 ml chilli and garlic sauce
pepper to taste

Preheat the oven to 180 °C (350 °F). Spray a round, medium ovenproof dish with non-stick spray.

Arrange the boerewors in a spiral and fry in a heated pan till brown and done. Remove and set aside.

Blend the mealie meal with 125 ml water. Heat the remaining water in a saucepan and add the blended mealie meal when the water comes to the boil. Add a pinch of salt and stir till the porridge comes to the boil and thickens. Simmer till done. Stir in a little Cheddar cheese, reserving the rest to sprinkle on top.

Turn the porridge into the prepared dish. Still keeping the boerewors in a spiral, place it on top of the porridge.

Heat the tomato and onion mix and chilli and garlic sauce together. Season to taste with salt and pepper and simmer for about 5 minutes. Spoon some of the sauce over the boerewors and sprinkle with the remaining cheese. Bake for 15-20 minutes or till heated through.

Serve with the remaining sauce.

Serves 4-6.

Sausage with herb crust

Cottage pie with sausage

Sausage with herb crust

Mrs Mostert of Bracken Downs, Alberton, covers fried sausage with a herb crust to transform it into a satisfying meal.

500 g thin mutton sausage
1 large onion, finely chopped
2 large, ripe tomatoes, skinned and diced
salt and black pepper to taste
5 ml origanum

Topping
100 g (170 ml) self-raising flour
5 ml salt
5 ml mixed herbs
100 g (250 ml) Cheddar cheese, grated
1 extra-large egg
150 ml milk
15 ml oil

Preheat the oven to 180 °C (350 °F). Spray a 20-cm ovenproof dish with non-stick spray.

Fry the sausage in a pan till brown on both sides. Roll the sausage into a spiral and place it in the prepared dish. Sauté the onion in the pan fat till soft and add the diced tomatoes. Add the seasonings and simmer till a nice sauce has formed. Pour the sauce over the sausage.

Mix all the topping ingredients. Spoon on top of the sausage and bake for about 20 minutes or till baked through and lightly browned on top.

Serve with a green salad.

Serves 4-6.

Cottage pie with sausage

The sausage in this cottage pie is first covered with a layer of baked beans in tomato sauce and then topped with a layer of mashed potato. Jeanette Ackermann of Parys says it's one of her favourite standbys, especially when she has to make a meal in a hurry.

500 g sausage
1 onion, finely chopped
1 can (410 g) baked beans in tomato sauce
750 ml mashed potato

Preheat the oven to 180 °C (350 °F).

Arrange the sausage in a spiral in a pan with an ovenproof handle or in an ovenproof dish. Sprinkle the onion on top. Bake in the oven till the sausage is brown and done. Spoon the baked beans in tomato sauce on top and top with layer of mashed potato. For a decorative effect, pipe the mashed potato on top of the baked beans. Return the dish to the oven and bake till the potato just begins to brown. Serve with a salad.

Serves 4.

Bully beef loaf

Bully beef is a great standby when the meat supply in the freezer is low. The whole hard-boiled eggs in the centre give the loaf a very attractive appearance when sliced. Mrs Cynthia Crook of Primrose serves the loaf with peas and potatoes or with a green salad.

4 x 250 ml fresh breadcrumbs
2 onions, finely chopped
oil
2 cans (300 g each) bully beef, mashed
5 ml dried sage
50 ml finely chopped parsley
few drops Tabasco sauce
salt and black pepper to taste
2 eggs, lightly beaten
about 75 ml milk
4 hard-boiled eggs, shelled

Preheat the oven to 180 °C (350 ° F). Grease a 23 x 13 x 7-cm

Bully beef loaf

Bully beef pie

loaf tin with margarine. Sprinkle a little of the fresh breadcrumbs in the bottom of the tin.

Sauté the onion in a little heated oil till soft. Combine with the bully beef and remaining breadcrumbs. Add the seasoning and mix.

Beat the eggs and milk together and add enough of the mixture to the bully beef mixture to bind it well.

Spoon half the bully beef mixture into the prepared tin, spreading it evenly. Place the hard-boiled eggs on top. Spoon the remaining bully beef mixture on top and spread evenly. Cover with tin foil and bake for about 45-60 minutes or till the loaf is done and firm. Cool slightly in the tin before carefully turning out onto a serving platter.

Serves 6.

Bully beef pie

Tertia du Toit of Bellville makes this quick pie in the microwave oven.

4 slices white or brown bread, crusts removed
butter or margarine
prepared mustard or wholegrain mustard
1 onion, finely chopped
5 ml margarine or butter
1 can (300 g) bully beef, cut into pieces
2 eggs
250 ml milk
salt and black pepper
little grated Cheddar cheese
paprika

Cut the slices of bread diagonally to form triangles and butter both sides of the triangles. Spread one side with mustard and arrange in a glass dish with the mustard side facing up.

Place the onion and 5 ml margarine in a small glass bowl and cover with plastic wrap. Prick the plastic wrap. Microwave the onion and butter for 1½ minutes on 100% power. Mix with the bully beef and spoon onto the bread.

Whisk the eggs and milk together, season lightly with salt and black pepper and pour over the ingredients in the glass dish. Sprinkle with a little Cheddar cheese and a little paprika. Cover with plastic wrap and microwave for 7 minutes on 50% power and thereafter for 5-8 minutes on 70% power or till the egg mixture has set. Leave for about 5 minutes before serving.

Serves 3-4.

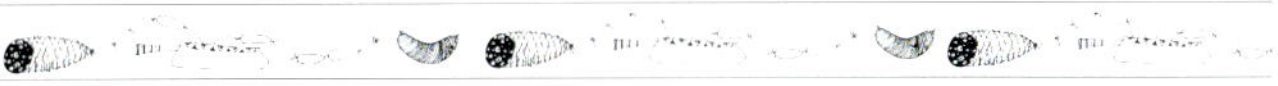

HOW TO FREEZE COOKED MEAT

- Always be scrupulously hygienic when preparing meat.
- Reduce the cooking time of dishes by 15-30 minutes (the average warming-up time).
- Cool the cooked dish completely before transferring it to containers for freezing.
- Avoid ingredients which do not freeze well like pasta, potatoes and rice.
- Avoid garnishings like parsley, lettuce or celery which become limp when frozen.
- Avoid strong seasonings like curry and pepper as freezing affects their flavour.
- Add salt when reheating the dish.
- Limit the use of cream and fat since it easily separates when reheated.

Bully beef surprise

Ideal for a quick meal, writes Mrs T Armstrong of Kensington, Johannesburg.

125 g bacon, cut into small pieces
2 cloves garlic, crushed
2 potatoes, peeled and diced
2 large ripe tomatoes, skinned and finely chopped
250 ml chicken stock
1 can (300 g) bully beef, diced
2 ml mixed herbs
salt and pepper to taste
4 slices toast, buttered and cut into fingers

Fry the bacon till done but not crisp.

Add the garlic and diced potato and stir-fry for about 1 minute. Add the tomato and stock, reduce the heat and simmer till the potato is nearly done. Add the remaining ingredients, except the toast. Simmer for about 5 minutes or till the mixture is heated through.

Serve with the buttered toast fingers.

Serves 4.

Bully beef surprise

Bully beef and bean scone wheels

A generous and filling recipe. The scone roll is made with beans in tomato sauce, bully beef and onion and tomato mix. Phillistas M Seboane of Jane Furse Hospital cuts the scone roll into wheels and arranges the slices in a dish before baking. Alternatively, bake the roll as is.

Filling
1 can (410 g) baked beans in tomato sauce
1 can (410 g) onion and tomato mix
1 can (300 g) bully beef
5 ml basil
salt and pepper to taste
100 g (250 ml) Cheddar cheese, grated

Scone dough
750 g (5 x 250 ml + 90 ml) self-raising flour
2 ml salt
5 ml mustard powder
180 g margarine
2 extra-large eggs
about 350 ml buttermilk or sour milk

Preheat the oven to 200 °C (400 °F). Grease a baking sheet or large oven dish with margarine.

Mix all the ingredients for the filling, except the cheese. Set aside.

Combine all the dry ingredients for the dough. Grate in the margarine and rub in with your fingertips till well blended. Whisk the eggs and buttermilk together and add just enough of the liquid to form a soft manageable dough. Mix with a spatula till just blended. On a floured surface, roll out the dough till about 7 mm thick. Spread the filling on top of the dough and sprinkle with the Cheddar cheese. Roll up the dough, divide the roll in half and place on the prepared baking sheet or slice the dough into 2-cm thick slices and arrange in the ovenproof dish. Bake for 15-20 minutes or till done.

Serve with a salad.

Serves 6-8.

Bully beef and bean scone wheels

Bully beef crumble

Bully beef crumble

Mrs M Minty of Burgersdorp serves bully beef and vegetables with a white sauce and tops the mixture with a crumbed crust.

1 onion, finely chopped
25 ml butter or margarine
1 tomato, skinned and finely chopped
400 g mixed vegetables
1 can (300 g) bully beef, cut into pieces
salt and black pepper to taste

White sauce
25 ml margarine
50 ml cake flour
350 ml milk
pinch nutmeg

Crumbed crust
25 ml margarine
250 ml cake flour
2 ml salt

Preheat the oven to 180 °C (350 °F). Grease an ovenproof dish with margarine.

Sauté the onion in the butter till soft. Add the tomato and simmer till soft. Stir in the mixed vegetables and bully beef and season to taste with salt and black pepper.

Prepare a white sauce using the margarine, cake flour and milk. Season with salt and pepper and nutmeg. Mix with the bully beef mixture and spoon into the prepared dish.

Rub the margarine, cake flour and salt together till crumbly. Sprinkle over the bully beef and bake for about 15-20 minutes till the crust is pale brown and the dish is warmed through.

Serves 4.

Creamy kidneys

Liver and kidneys

Creamy kidneys

This is one of many recipes in her grandmother's recipe book which she inherited, writes Chantelle Liebenberg of Warrenton.

Instead of making potato rosettes to serve with the creamy kidneys, you can serve the kidneys in potato nests or with mashed potato.

6 potatoes
little milk and butter
salt and freshly ground black pepper to taste
1 onion, chopped
oil
6 sheep's kidneys, membrane and tubes removed and soaked in salted water
125 ml milk
20-30 ml chutney

Boil the potatoes in salted water till soft. Remove the skins and mash the potatoes with a little milk and butter. Season with salt. Pipe rosettes or shape the potato into nests on a baking sheet and grill for a few minutes till the peaks are slightly browned. Set aside.

Sauté the onion in a little oil till soft. Drain the kidneys, cut into smaller pieces and season with salt and black pepper. Fry the kidneys in a little oil till brown on the outside and still slightly pink inside. Add the milk and the chutney and simmer for a few minutes till the sauce thickens slightly. Season with extra salt and pepper if necessary, and serve with the potato rosettes or spoon into the potato nests.

Serves 4-6.

Liver pie

Jill van Eck of Henley on Klip uses liver, kidneys and heart to make this pie, but we made it with only liver and kidneys.

750 g sheep's liver and sheep's kidneys
nutmeg, ginger and salt and pepper to taste
cake flour for rolling in
4 rashers bacon
3 stalks celery, sliced into rings
oil for frying
500 ml chicken stock
75 g (125 ml) seedless raisins
30 ml finely chopped parsley
5 ml rosemary (optional)
2-3 bay leaves
400 g puff pastry
1 egg yolk, whisked

Preheat the oven to 200 °C (400 °F). Spray a 26-cm ovenproof pie dish with non-stick spray.

Clean the liver and kidneys. Remove the membranes and all the tough parts. Cut the liver and kidneys into 2-cm cubes. Season with nutmeg, ginger, and salt and pepper to taste. Roll the cubes in the cake flour.

Fry the bacon till crisp and chop coarsely. Sauté the celery in the bacon fat till soft and remove from the pan. Fry the cubed liver and kidneys in the heated oil till brown. Reduce the heat and slowly add the chicken stock. Return the bacon and celery to the pan. Add the raisins, parsley, rosemary and bay leaves. Simmer till the sauce thickens and turn the mixture into the prepared pie dish.

Roll out the puff pastry on a floured surface and place on top of the mixture in the pie dish. Trim the edges, cut out leaves from the remaining pastry and use to decorate the crust. Brush the entire pastry crust with whisked egg yolk. Bake for 25-30 minutes or till the crust is baked and golden brown on top.

Serve with mashed potato and vegetables.

Serves 6-8.

Liver pie

Chicken livers with potato

Chicken livers with potato

Naomi Erlank of Nylstroom serves this dish on bread or with rice.

1 large onion, finely chopped
oil
500 g chicken livers, cleaned
salt and freshly ground black pepper to taste
3 large potatoes, peeled and thinly sliced
chicken stock

Sauté the onion in a little oil till soft. Season the chicken livers with salt and pepper and fry till brown on the outside but still slightly pink inside. Add the potatoes and a little chicken stock and simmer till the potatoes are soft and done.

Serves 2-3.

Tomato chicken livers

Chicken livers with tomato is her brother-in-law's favourite dish, writes Mrs Reinette van der Zwan of Honeydew.

500 g chicken livers, cleaned
salt and freshly ground black pepper to taste
oil
1 onion, sliced
1 green pepper, seeded and diced
200 g mushrooms, sliced (optional)
oil for frying
2 ripe tomatoes, skinned and diced
100 ml tomato sauce
25-50 ml Worcester sauce

Season the chicken livers with salt and pepper and fry in heated oil till brown. Remove from the pan and set aside.

Sauté the onion and green pepper in the same pan till soft. Add the mushrooms and stir-fry till pale brown. Add the tomatoes. Blend the tomato and Worcester sauce, add to the mixture in the pan and simmer till the tomato is soft. Return the chicken livers to the mixture and simmer till the dish is heated through. Season with salt and pepper, if necessary.

Serve with rice.

Serves 3-4.

Chicken liver delight

Chicken liver delight

Drienie Olivier of Klerksdorp has all kinds of tasty ideas with chicken livers. She prepares them with onion, curries them or adds flavour with a sweet-and-sour sauce. She serves the chicken livers with rice or mashed potato.

BASIC RECIPE
1 onion, sliced
oil
500 g chicken livers, cleaned
salt and freshly ground black pepper to taste
chopped parsley

Sauté the onion in a little oil till soft. Season the chicken livers with salt and pepper, add to the onion and fry till brown on the outside but still slightly pink inside.

Serve with a sprinkling of freshly chopped parsely and mashed potato or rice. Alternatively, serve the chicken livers with a sweet-and-sour sauce or curry them.

Serves 2-3.

SWEET-AND-SOUR SAUCE
100 ml white grape vinegar
80 g (100 ml) sugar
15 ml soy sauce
7 ml cornflour, blended with a little cold water

Prepare the chicken livers as described in the basic recipe. Blend the grape vinegar and sugar and add to the cooked chicken liver mixture. Reduce the heat and simmer for about 2 minutes. Blend the soy sauce with the cornflour and add to the chicken liver mixture. Heat till the sauce comes to the boil and thickens. Stir frequently.

Serve warm.

Serves 2-3.

CURRY MIXTURE
5 ml curry
2 ml ground cumin (jeera)
2 ml ground coriander
2 ml turmeric
5 ml sugar
15-30 ml grape vinegar

Prepare the chicken livers as described in the basic recipe. Mix all the ingredients for the curry mixture and add to the cooked chicken liver mixture.

Simmer for about 2 minutes or till heated through. Add a little water, if necessary.

Serve with rice, chutney and banana slices.

Serves 2-3.

BUYING HINTS

- Buy meat in bulk. The price per kilogram of half or a whole slaughter animal is usually much less than the total price of all the individual cuts. When buying meat in bulk you pay the same price for mince, roasts and steaks. It is also easier to determine portion sizes and to plan your menus in advance.
- Compare the prices of different cuts of meat and also compare the prices at different meat markets. Then buy the best quality for the best price, always keeping your family's likes and dislikes in mind.
- Make use of special offers, provided the meat cuts satisfy your specific needs and you have adequate refrigeration and freezing facilities.
- Compare the price per portion rather than the price per kilogram. Meat with a minimum bone and fat content may be more expensive per kilogram, but may still cost less per portion.

  Also compare the price per edible portion with the price of other protein sources.
- Avoid making your purchases during peak times like the end of the month or over Christmas.
- Chat to your butcher: He is there to help you with your purchases and has years of experience in the choice and preparation of meat.

  Also ask you meat dealer to prepare certain cuts for you. So, for example, he can prepare meat rolls, strips for stir-fries, beef olives, mince, etc.
- Freeze meat in meal-size portions to ensure that unnecessary big portions are not being used.

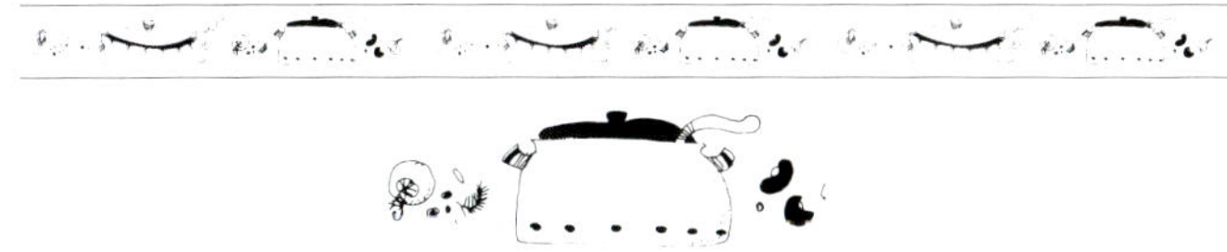

Tomato chicken livers

Chicken and sweet potato potjie

Scrumptious chicken

Chicken and sweet potato potjie

This potjie can also be made with pork shank or neck, writes Elna de Klerk of Bellville. Pour all leftover wine, red and white mixed, in a bottle and use for dishes similar to this one. Otherwise use box wine rather than specially opening a good bottle of white wine for cooking.

2 large onions, sliced
2 stalks celery, sliced
3 cloves garlic, crushed
oil
8 chicken thighs
salt and pepper to taste
5 large sweet potatoes, skinned and sliced into rings
8 carrots, scraped and cut into pieces
200 g dried apricots (optional)
250 ml white wine
10 ml soy sauce
75 ml soft brown sugar
15 ml tomato sauce or mustard sauce (the sweet-and-sour brand)
10 ml basil

Sauté the onion, celery and garlic in a little oil till soft. Season the chicken thighs with salt and pepper, add and fry till brown.

Arrange the vegetables in layers on top of the meat. End with a layer of apricots. Blend the white wine, soy sauce, brown sugar, tomato or mustard sauce and basil and pour over the dish. Cover, reduce the heat and simmer till the chicken and vegetables are tender and done. Do not stir the potjie; just scrape the bottom of the pot every now and then with a spatula to ensure that the food does not stick. Season to taste with salt and pepper.

Serve with hot bread.

Serves 8.

Chicken stew

The more sauce there is, the further a stew goes. Chicken is a real standby when it comes to making economical dishes and stews. Serve this dish with rice, writes Mrs Dee Smith of Quigrey, East London.

1 whole chicken, cut into pieces
salt and pepper
oil for frying
2 onions, sliced
2 cloves garlic, crushed
10 ml mild curry powder
2 large, ripe tomatoes, skinned and diced
1 packet (15 g) tomato soup powder
500 ml chicken stock
10 ml mixed herbs
5-7 ml basil
pinch nutmeg
20 ml tomato purée
10 ml sugar
4 potatoes, halved
4 carrots, chopped
20 ml parsley, finely chopped

Season the chicken pieces well with salt and pepper and brown in the heated oil. Remove from the pan and set aside.

Sauté the onion and garlic in the oil in the pan till soft. Add the curry powder and stir-fry for about 1 minute. Add the tomatoes and simmer till the mixture forms a purée.

Blend the tomato soup powder and chicken stock and add. Season with all the seasonings. Return the chicken pieces to the sauce. Simmer till the chicken is nearly done and tender. Add the potatoes and carrots and simmer till the chicken and vegetables are done and the sauce has thickened. Sprinkle with parsley and serve with rice.

Serves 4-6.

Chicken stew

Delicious chicken

Delicious chicken

Her family and friends always ask her for this recipe, writes Mrs Joey Jooste of Môrewag, Kroonstad. The dish is a meal-in-one and contains all the ingredients for a well-balanced meal. Serve with a mixed salad, suggests Mrs Jooste.

1 whole chicken, cut into pieces or 8 chicken pieces
salt and black pepper to taste
oil
500 ml chicken stock
1 onion, coarsely chopped
1 green pepper, coarsely chopped (optional)
30 ml margarine
30 ml cake flour
about 200 ml milk
5 ml mustard powder
250-500 ml cooked rice
125 ml peas
50 g (125 ml) Cheddar cheese, grated (optional)

Preheat the oven to 180 °C (350 °F).

Season the chicken pieces to taste with salt and black pepper. Brown the meat in the heated oil. Add the chicken stock and simmer till the chicken is tender and done. Drain the stock and reserve. Remove the chicken from the saucepan and debone it, if preferred. Heat a little more oil in the pan and sauté the onion and green pepper till soft. Remove from the pan.

Melt the margarine in the pan. Add the cake flour and stir till a smooth paste is formed. Heat till the cake flour is cooked, stirring continuously. Add enough milk to the chicken stock to make up 500 ml. Slowly add the chicken stock mixture to the cake flour mixture while stirring continuously. Heat, stirring continuously, till the mixture comes to the boil and thickens. Season with the mustard powder and salt and pepper to taste.

Combine the rice, peas, onion and green pepper and spoon into an ovenproof dish. Place the chicken pieces on top and pour over the sauce. Sprinkle with the Cheddar cheese and heat in the oven till the cheese has melted and the dish is heated through.

Serve with a salad.

Serves 6-8.

Chicken casserole with chutney

Asparagus and chicken casserole

Chicken casserole with chutney

Served with rice and vegetables, this chicken casserole with chutney is a real winner, writes Miss Sally Lenton of Lobatse.

1,2 kg chicken pieces, cleaned
salt and black pepper
oil
4 potatoes, skinned and sliced
150-175 ml chutney
500 ml milk
20 ml mild curry powder
1 can (410 g) cream of chicken soup

Preheat the oven to 180 °C (350 °F).

Lightly season the chicken pieces with salt and black pepper and brown in a little heated oil. Place in an ovenproof dish and arrange the potato slices between the pieces.

Blend all the ingredients for the sauce and pour the mixture over the chicken.

Cover and bake for about 1 hour or till the chicken is tender and done.

Serves 8-10.

HINT

• Add more chicken to the casserole if you find there is too much gravy.

Asparagus and chicken casserole

Miss Caeleen McNaughton of Cindapark, Boksburg, serves a green salad with this chicken dish. It serves a large number of people and requires very little preparation.

120 g (2 x 250 ml) fresh breadcrumbs
100 g (250 ml) Cheddar cheese, grated
1,2 kg chicken pieces, cleaned
salt and black pepper
oil
1 can (430 g) asparagus salad cuts
1 can (425 g) cream of asparagus soup
125 ml chicken stock
5-7 ml mustard powder

Preheat the oven to 180 °C (350 °F). Grease an ovenproof dish with margarine.

Combine the breadcrumbs and Cheddar cheese. Sprinkle half the mixture into the prepared dish.

Season the chicken pieces lightly with salt and black pepper and brown in a little heated oil. Arrange in the ovenproof dish.

Drain the asparagus salad cuts, reserving the liquid. Arrange the asparagus on top of the chicken pieces. Blend the liquid with the asparagus soup, chicken stock and mustard powder. Pour over the chicken pieces.

Sprinkle the remaining breadcrumbs and Cheddar cheese on top, cover with tin foil and bake for about 1 hour or till the chicken is tender and done. Remove the tin foil after about 40 minutes.

Serves 8-10.

Leftover chicken with herb crust

Top chicken, pork or mince with this herb crust. The recipe was sent in by Mrs Elna de Klerk of Oakdale, Bellville.

1 chicken (about 1,2 kg), cooked till the meat falls off the bone

SAUCE

1 packet (48 g) brown onion soup powder
15 ml mustard powder
250 ml water
25 ml white grape vinegar
25 ml white wine
15 ml soy sauce
30 ml golden syrup
30 ml tomato sauce

HERB BATTER

1 extra-large egg
160 ml buttermilk
125 ml oil
140 g (250 ml) cake flour
10 ml baking powder
3 ml salt
5 ml sugar
3 ml mixed herbs
2 ml aniseed

Leftover chicken with herb crust

Preheat the oven to 180 °C (350 °F).

Cut the chicken into bite-size pieces. Set aside.

Combine the brown onion soup powder and mustard powder in a saucepan. Add the water and blend well till smooth. Add the remaining sauce ingredients. Heat, stirring continuously, till the sauce comes to the boil and thickens. Add the chicken and simmer till the meat is heated through. Pour into an ovenproof dish.

Beat the egg, buttermilk and oil together.

In a large mixing bowl, sift together the cake flour, baking powder and salt. Add the sugar, mixed herbs and aniseed and mix well. Add the egg mixture and beat with a wire beater till well blended. Pour over the chicken mixture and bake for 35-40 minutes or till the crust is baked through and golden brown and puffed out.

Serve immediately with a mixed salad.

Serves 4-6.

HINT

• Any leftover vegetables like peas, carrots or mushrooms can be added to the meat.

Chicken bobotie

Bobotie made with chicken is a delicious change from traditional bobotie. The rice is also mixed into the bobotie, so you need only serve sambals and perhaps a mixed salad with this dish. Mrs Hesca Crafford of Magalieskruin sent us the recipe.

YELLOW RICE

200 g (250 ml) rice
600 ml boiling water
75 g (125 ml) raisins
30 ml sugar
2 ml turmeric
2 ml mild curry powder
salt to taste

CHICKEN MIXTURE

1 whole chicken, about 1,2 kg
400 ml chicken stock
freshly ground black pepper to taste
1 onion, sliced
2 cloves garlic, crushed
oil
15 ml mild curry powder
5 ml turmeric
5 ml coriander
3 ml ground cumin (jeera)
5 ml chicken spice
45 ml chutney
15 ml lemon juice

TOPPING

125 ml milk
2 extra-large eggs

Preheat the oven to 180 °C (350 °F). Spray a 26 x 22 x 6-cm ovenproof dish with non-stick spray.

Place all ingredients for the yellow rice in a saucepan and boil till the rice is cooked and soft. Drain and set aside.

Cut the chicken into pieces and rinse. Place the chicken pieces in a large saucepan, pour over the chicken stock and season with freshly ground black pepper. Boil till the chicken is cooked and tender, and the meat easily falls off the bone. Debone the chicken and cut the meat into bite-size pieces.

Sauté the onion and garlic in oil till soft. Add the curry powder, turmeric, coriander, cumin and chicken spice and stir-fry for about 1 minute.

Add the chicken as well as the remaining seasonings and mix well. Heat well.

Add the cooked yellow rice to the mixture and mix well. Turn into the prepared dish.

Beat the milk and eggs together and pour over the chicken mixture. Make a few holes in the chicken mixture with a fork to allow the egg mixture to spread evenly. Bake for 20-30 minutes or till the egg mixture has set.

Serves 6-8.

Chicken bobotie

Spaghetti with baked beans

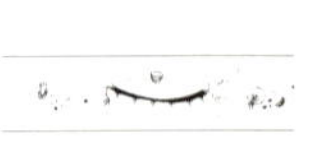

Passion for pasta

Spaghetti with baked beans

A good standby for the end of the month when your grocery supplies are running low, writes S D Ogle of Mariannhill.

125 g bacon
1 onion, finely chopped
4-6 cloves garlic, crushed
15 ml masala
1 tomato, skinned and coarsely chopped
1 can (410 g) baked beans in tomato sauce
salt to taste
1 packet (500 g) spaghetti, cooked
parsley for sprinkling on top (optional)

Fry the bacon in the pan till done but not crisp. Add the onion and garlic and stir-fry till the onion is soft. Add the masala and stir-fry for about 1 minute. Add the tomato and simmer till the mixture forms a purée.

Stir in the baked beans and heat till warmed through. Stir occasionally and season with salt to taste.

Spoon the spaghetti onto a serving platter and spoon the sauce on top. Sprinkle with parsley, if preferred.

Serves 4.

Spaghetti with chicken livers and pineapple

Try frying one or two rashers bacon with the onion till crisp, keeping in mind that this will add to the cost of the dish. Miss K A Glynn of Lüderitz, Namibia sent in the recipe.

1 onion, sliced
2 cloves garlic, crushed
oil
2 containers (250 g each) chicken livers, cut into smaller pieces
1 tomato, skinned and diced
15 ml cake flour
250 ml milk
1 can (260 g) pineapple chunks, drained, reserve the juice
10 ml tomato paste (optional)
salt and pepper to taste
basil to taste
½ packet (250 g) spaghetti
grated Cheddar cheese to sprinkle on top (optional)

Sauté the onion and garlic in a little oil till soft. Add the chicken livers and fry till browned but still slightly pink inside. Add the tomato and fry till soft.

Blend the cake flour with a little of the milk to form a paste and set aside. Add the remaining milk to the chicken liver mixture. Add a little of the pineapple juice, if preferred. Add the pineapple chunks and heat slowly till heated through. Add the cake flour paste and stir continuously till the mixture comes to the boil and thickens. Add the tomato paste, if preferred. Season well with salt and pepper and basil to taste.

Cook the spaghetti in rapidly boiling salted water till just done. Drain and transfer to a serving dish. Serve immediately with the chicken liver mixture and grated Cheddar cheese, if preferred.

Serves 4.

Spaghetti with chicken livers and pineapple

Spaghetti with pork

Spaghetti with pork

The longer this pasta dish is left to stand, the better the flavour, writes Mrs Tertia Nel of Paarl.

¼-½ packet (125-250 g) spaghetti
6 rashers bacon (optional)
oil (optional)
2 onions, sliced
2 cloves garlic, crushed
125-250 ml chopped celery (optional)
500-750 g pork stewing meat, cubed
salt and freshly ground black pepper
10 ml ginger
10 ml ground coriander
30 ml soy sauce
chicken stock or hot water
500 g green beans, cut into 2-cm pieces and cooked till just tender

Cook the spaghetti in rapidly boiling salted water till soft. Drain well and set aside.

Fry the optional bacon till crisp and remove from the pan. Dice and set aside.

Add a little oil to the pan, if the bacon were not used, and sauté the onion, garlic and celery till soft. Remove from the pan and set aside.

Season the pork to taste with salt and pepper as well as with half the ginger and coriander. Brown the meat. Add the soy sauce and mix well. Pour over a little chicken stock or hot water, reduce the heat and simmer till the meat is tender. Add the onion mixture as well as the green beans and bacon and season with the remaining seasonings. Stir-fry till hot.

Spoon on top of the spaghetti and mix lightly. Heat through and serve with slices of fried banana, if preferred.

Serves 6-8.

Spaghetti with bully beef

Spaghetti with egg and bacon (1)

Spaghetti with bully beef

Serve this dish hot or cold, writes Mrs Sarie de Villiers of Witfield. When serving it cold as a salad, Mrs De Villiers likes to use shell noodles.

2 onions, finely chopped
1 green pepper, diced
oil
1 can (300 g) bully beef, diced
3 tomatoes, skinned and chopped
1 can (410 g) cream-style sweetcorn
5 ml basil
pinch sugar
salt and freshly ground black pepper
½ packet (250 g) spaghetti
grated Cheddar cheese (optional)

Sauté the onion and green pepper in a little oil till soft. Add the bully beef and stir-fry till pale brown. Add the chopped tomatoes and simmer till soft. Stir in the cream-style sweetcorn and season with basil, sugar and salt and freshly ground black pepper to taste.

In the meantime, cook the spaghetti in rapidly boiling salted water till just soft. Drain and mix with the bully beef mixture. Serve with grated Cheddar cheese, if preferred.

Serves 6.

VARIATIONS

• Instead of bully beef, use 500 ml cooked chicken, or 125 g bacon or even 6-8 Vienna sausages.

Spaghetti with egg and bacon (1)

You can add a variety of extras to this quick and easy dish to transform it into something different every time you make it, writes Karin Augustyn of Ladysmith.

½ packet (250 g) spaghetti
250 g bacon, chopped into small pieces or bacon offcuts
4 extra-large eggs, beaten
80 g (200 ml) Cheddar cheese, grated
salt and freshly ground black pepper to taste

Cook the spaghetti in rapidly boiling salted water till soft. Drain well and set aside.

Fry the bacon in a pan till crisp, adding a little oil if necessary. Add the spaghetti to the bacon in the pan and mix.

Mix the eggs with three quarters of the Cheddar cheese. Remove the pan from the heat and stir the egg mixture into the spaghetti mixture. Stir till well blended and the cheese has melted slightly – the heat from the pan will be sufficient to cook the egg. Season well with salt and black pepper and serve immediately. Serve extra cheese in a separate bowl for sprinkling on top.

Serves 4.

VARIATION

• You can fry any one of the following with the bacon: sliced mushrooms, onions or courgettes; left-over cooked chicken, vegetables or Vienna sausages.

Spaghetti with egg and bacon (2)

Similar to the previous recipe, except for the addition of some garlic. She was given this recipe by an Italian who lives in Rome, writes Mrs Gisela Botha of Vlaeberg. It has become one of her favourite dishes.

½ packet (250 g) spaghetti
250 g streaky bacon, cut into pieces
3 cloves garlic, crushed
olive oil
5 eggs, lightly whisked
salt and black pepper to taste
100 g (250 ml) Cheddar cheese, grated
Parmesan cheese (optional)

Cook the spaghetti in rapidly boiling salted water till soft. Drain and set aside.

Fry the bacon and crushed garlic in a little olive oil till the bacon is cooked but not crisp. Add the spaghetti and mix. Season the eggs with salt and black pepper and stir into the spaghetti mixture. Continue stirring with a fork till the egg coats the spaghetti. Stir in the cheese, heating till the cheese has melted and the egg is done.

Serve with Parmesan cheese, if preferred, and a salad.

Serves 4-6.

Spaghetti with egg and bacon (2)

Spaghetti with cabbage and chicken

Curried cabbage served with spaghetti makes a tasty supper, writes Elize Geldenhuys of Stellenbosch.

½ packet (250 g) spaghetti
1 onion, sliced into rings
2 leeks, sliced into rings
2 cloves garlic, crushed
oil
10 ml ground ginger
10 ml curry powder
600 g chicken breasts, deboned and sliced in strips
400 g (about a ¼) cabbage, shredded
60 ml tomato sauce
salt and black pepper to taste

Cook the spaghetti in rapidly boiling salted water till just soft. Drain and set aside.

Sauté the sliced onion, leek and garlic in a little oil till soft. Add the ginger and curry powder and stir-fry for about 1 minute. Add the chicken strips and stir-fry till done, but not dry. Add the cabbage and stir-fry till the cabbage is just tender but still crisp. Add the spaghetti and mix. Add the tomato sauce, mix and heat till warmed through.

Season to taste with salt and black pepper.

Serves 4-5.

Chicken with spaghetti

Chicken, spaghetti and a red wine sauce makes for a deliciously filling and nourishing meal. Mrs E Walsh of Windsorpark, Kraaifontein arranges the spaghetti and sauce in layers and sprinkles the dish with Cheddar cheese. She serves the chicken pieces separately but we added them to the sauce.

4 rashers bacon, chopped
1 large onion, sliced
1 green pepper, seeded and diced
1 packet (200 g) button mushrooms, sliced
1 can (410 g) tomato purée
250 ml dry red wine
30 ml Worcester sauce
pinch ground cloves
5 ml allspice
pinch nutmeg
10 ml paprika
15 ml sugar
salt and black pepper to taste
about 1 kg cooked chicken, deboned and cut into pieces
1 packet (500 g) spaghetti, boiled till soft
Cheddar cheese for sprinkling (optional)

Fry the bacon till done, add the onion, green pepper and mushrooms and sauté till soft. Add the tomato purée, red wine and seasonings and simmer to form a flavoursome sauce. Add the chicken pieces and simmer till heated through.

Serve the spaghetti, sauce and Cheddar cheese separately.

Serves 6.

Spaghetti with cabbage and chicken

Chicken with spaghetti

Pasta with sour cream sauce

Just before serving, Mrs Sylvia Hayes of Durbanville stirs a little Cheddar cheese into this bacon and sour cream sauce to make it even richer, but it tastes just as good without.

125-250 g bacon
1 onion, coarsely chopped
3 cloves garlic, crushed
oil
1 tomato, skinned and cut into pieces
250 ml sour cream
1 packet (500 g) spaghetti, cooked

Fry the bacon in a pan till done but not crisp. Remove from the pan and cut into smaller pieces.

Sauté the onion and garlic in the pan till soft, adding more oil if necessary. Add the tomato and simmer till a purée is formed. Add the bacon pieces and sour cream and simmer till the sauce thickens slightly.

Transfer the cooked and drained spaghetti to a serving dish and pour over the sauce just before serving.

Serves 4-6.

Creamy tomato sauce spaghetti

Serve spaghetti with a sauce made with a can of tomato soup. Add Cheddar cheese to make it even more flavoursome and creamy. The recipe was sent in by Jeanette Memela of KwaXuma.

½ packet (250 g) spaghetti
125-250 g bacon, cut into pieces, if preferred
1 onion, finely chopped
1 can (405 g) tomato soup
125 ml cream
125 ml water
1 ml salt
1 ml cayenne pepper
black pepper to taste
Cheddar cheese for sprinkling on top

Preheat the oven to 180 °C (350 °F).

Boil the spaghetti in plenty of rapidly boiling salted water till just soft. Drain and turn into an ovenproof dish.

Fry the bacon in a pan till done but not crisp. Remove from the pan and mix with the spaghetti.

Sauté the onion in the pan fat till soft. Add the tomato soup, cream and water and heat slowly while stirring continuously till the sauce comes to the boil. Season with salt, cayenne pepper and black pepper to taste. Pour over the spaghetti and mix. Sprinkle with a little cheese and heat in the oven till the dish is warmed through and the cheese has melted.

Serve with a salad.

Serves 6.

Spaghetti with spinach

Mary Doo of Somerset West makes a substantial dish with spinach and spaghetti. Sprinkle with cheese, if preferred and serve with a green salad, although the dish itself is so nourishing a salad isn't even necessary. Sometimes she adds a little chopped bacon when sautéing the onion, writes Mrs Doo.

1 large onion, sliced into rings
1 clove garlic, crushed
2 stalks celery, sliced into rings
oil
1 packet (250 g) button mushrooms, sliced (optional)
2 bunches (300 g each) spinach (stems removed), washed and shredded
1 can (410 g) tomato and onion mix or 1 can (410 g) whole tomatoes
salt and pepper to taste
sugar
nutmeg
1 packet (500 g) spaghetti, boiled till just soft
Cheddar or Parmesan cheese (optional)

Sauté the onion, garlic and celery in a little oil till soft. Add the mushrooms and stir-fry till pale brown. Add the spinach and stir-fry till soft. Add the tomato and onion mix and simmer till a nice sauce is formed. Season to taste with salt, pepper, a little sugar and a pinch of nutmeg.

Serve with the spaghetti and grated Cheddar cheese or Parmesan cheese, if preferred.

Serves 6.

Pasta with sour cream sauce

Creamy tomato sauce spaghetti

Spaghetti with spinach

Macaroni with meatballs

Macaroni with sausage and potato

Lentil macaroni

Macaroni with meatballs

Mrs Anna Haasbroek of Soekmekaar was sorting through old recipes when she came across this one. It's easy to make and is ideal for supper, she says.

½ packet (250 g) macaroni
oil
1 onion, finely grated
2 stalks celery, chopped
100 g (250 ml) Cheddar cheese, grated
250 ml milk
2 eggs
salt and pepper
500 g mince
25 ml finely chopped parsley
1 tomato, slice

Preheat the oven to 180 °C (350 °F). Spray a 26 x 22-cm oven dish with non-stick spray.

Boil the macaroni till soft in rapidly boiling salted water to which a little oil has been added. Drain and set aside.

Sauté the onion and celery in a little oil till soft and mix with the macaroni. Add the Cheddar cheese and mix well. Turn into the prepared dish.

Beat the milk and eggs together, season with salt and pepper and pour over the macaroni mixture.

Season the mince with salt and pepper and add the parsley. Shape into fairly small meatballs. Arrange the tomato slices on top of the macaroni and place a meatball on top of each tomato slice. Bake for 45 minutes or till the meatballs are cooked and golden brown. Serve with a tomato sauce.

Serves 6.

Macaroni with sausage and potato

If you have a crowd for dinner use more potatoes to make the dish go further.

½ packet (250 g) macaroni
100 g (250 ml) Cheddar cheese, grated
50 ml finely chopped parsley
500 g boerewors
1 onion, finely chopped
1 large tomato, peeled and finely chopped
1-2 potatoes, peeled and thinly sliced
butter or garlic oil
salt and pepper
origanum

Preheat the oven to 180 ° (350 °F). Spray a deep 24-cm ovenproof dish with non-stick spray.

Cook the macaroni in rapidly boiling salted water till done. Drain well and spoon into the prepared dish. Sprinkle with half the cheese and parsley.

Fry the sausage in a pan till brown on both sides. Remove from the pan and arrange on top of the macaroni. Sauté the onion in the pan till soft and add the tomato. Simmer till soft and spoon over the sausage and macaroni. Top with the potato slices, dot with butter or garlic oil and season with salt and pepper and a little origanum. Sprinkle with the remaining cheese and parsley, cover and bake for 40-60 minutes or till the potato is done.

Serve with a salad.

Serves 4.

Lentil macaroni

A delicious variation on ordinary macaroni and cheese. Mrs Jan le Roux of Tsumeb says it's an ideal dish for vegetarians.

500 ml cooked brown lentils, well drained
1 tin (410 g) tomato and onion mix
1 clove garlic, crushed
5 ml basil
salt and pepper to taste
½ packet (250 g) macaroni
30 ml butter or margarine
30 ml cake flour
300 ml milk
5 ml mustard powder
100 g (250 ml) grated Cheddar cheese

Preheat the oven to 180 °C (350 °F). Grease an ovenproof dish with margarine.

Mix the lentils, tomato and onion mix and garlic together and season with basil, and salt and pepper to taste.

Boil the macaroni in rapidly boiling salted water till just soft. Drain.

Prepare a white sauce: Melt the butter and stir in the cake flour. Stir till smooth. Slowly add the milk. Heat, stirring continuously, till the sauce comes to the boil and thickens. Season with mustard powder, and salt and pepper to taste. Add some of the Cheddar cheese and mix. Spoon layers of macaroni, lentil mixture and white sauce into the ovenproof dish, ending with a layer of white sauce.

Sprinkle with the remaining cheese and bake for about 20-30 minutes or till the dish is heated through.

Serve with a salad.

Serves 6.

Bully beef and macaroni

A dish of macaroni cheese is always popular and can be varied in countless ways, as the letters sent in by our readers prove! One such a mouthwatering variation is this recipe sent in by Mrs Wilma Viljoen of Sasolburg. The dish has a white sauce base and is flavoured with herbs and tomatoes. The bully beef provides extra protein.

1 packet (500 g) elbow macaroni
salt
oil
1 onion, finely chopped
75 ml butter or margarine
75 ml cake flour
750 ml milk, slightly heated
salt and pepper to taste
2 large, ripe tomatoes, skinned and finely chopped
1 can (300 g) bully beef, diced
50 ml finely chopped parsley
50 ml chutney
10 ml mixed herbs
100 g (250 ml) Cheddar cheese, grated
50 ml fresh breadcrumbs

Preheat the oven to 180 °C (350 °F). Spray a large ovenproof dish with non-stick spray.

Cook the macaroni in rapidly boiling salted water to which a little oil has been added till just soft. Drain and set aside.

Sauté the onion in the heated butter till soft. Add the cake flour and stir well till the cake flour is smooth and all the lumps have disappeared. Remove from the heat and slowly add the milk while stirring continuously. Return the saucepan to the stove and heat till the mixture comes to the boil and thickens. Add the remaining ingredients except the breadcrumbs and only half the Cheddar cheese. Mix well. Spoon on top of the macaroni and mix well. Turn into the prepared dish.

Combine the remaining Cheddar cheese with the breadcrumbs and sprinkle on top. Bake for 20 minutes or till the cheese has melted.

Serve with a salad.

Serves 10-12.

Bully beef and macaroni

Noodles with tuna

Noodles with tuna

Mrs Veronica Hebler of Rietkuil writes that pasta lovers will enjoy this dish.

¼ packet (125 g) noodles
1 onion, finely chopped
2 cloves garlic, crushed
oil
2 tomatoes, skinned and diced
1 can (185 g) shredded tuna in brine
50 ml mayonnaise
25 ml chutney
salt and black pepper to taste
pinch nutmeg
few drops Tabasco sauce (optional)
sprinkling Cheddar cheese, grated
25 ml chopped parsley

Preheat the oven to 180 °C (350 °F). Grease an ovenproof dish with margarine.

Cook the noodles in rapidly boiling salted water till just soft. Drain and set aside. Sauté the onion and garlic in a little oil till soft. Add the diced tomato and simmer till the mixture forms a purée. Add the tuna and a little of the brine. Add the noodles, mayonnaise and chutney, blend and season with salt and black pepper, nutmeg and Tabasco sauce. Mix well and spoon into the prepared dish. Combine the Cheddar cheese and parsley and sprinkle on top.

Bake for about 20-30 minutes or till the cheese has melted and the dish is heated through.

Serve with a salad.

Serves 4.

Poor man's paella

Reliable rice dishes

Poor man's paella

She uses leftover chicken and rice to make her paella, writes Mrs Sharon Milligan of Sunward Park.

1 packet (375 g) Russian sausages, sliced
oil
1 large onion, finely chopped
7 ml mild curry powder
375 ml cooked rice
250 g leftover chicken, diced
500 g cooked haddock, flaked
125 ml frozen peas
125 ml frozen whole kernel corn
2 eggs, whisked
125 ml milk
salt and freshly ground black pepper
2 hard-boiled eggs, shelled and quartered

Fry the sausages in a little oil till brown. Remove from the pan and set aside. Fry the onion till soft, add the curry powder and stir-fry for 1 minute.

Add the cooked rice and stir-fry for 1 minute. Return the sausages to the pan, add the diced chicken and mix lightly. Add the flaked haddock, peas and corn and heat till the vegetables are defrosted and done.

Blend the whisked eggs and milk, stirring well. Pour over the paella and stir-fry till the eggs are done and set. Season to taste with salt and pepper.

Dish up on a serving platter and garnish with the hard-boiled eggs.

Serves 6.

Chicken paella

Paella is usually an expensive dish, but this version is economical because it is made without fish or seafood. The recipe was sent in by Mrs Jenny Bencini of Montclair, Durban.

1 whole chicken or 8 chicken pieces like breasts and thighs
salt and pepper to taste
oil
water or chicken stock
750 ml cooked yellow rice
1 onion, sliced
4 cloves garlic, crushed
1 green pepper, cut into strips
1 large, ripe tomato, skinned and diced
250 ml frozen peas
5 ml dried origanum
5 ml dried basil
pinch nutmeg
few drops Tabasco sauce

Season the chicken pieces with salt and pepper to taste and fry in the oil till brown. Add a little water or chicken stock, reduce the heat and simmer till the chicken is done. Remove from the pan and cool slightly. Debone and cut into bite-size pieces. (In the meantime, prepare the yellow rice [see hint underneath], by adding about 5 ml turmeric as well as salt to the water in which the rice is cooked.)

Sauté the onion, garlic and green pepper in a little oil till soft. Add the tomato and simmer till the tomato is soft. Add the chicken pieces and the peas. Stir-fry till heated through. Add the yellow rice and heat through, stirring frequently. Season with origanum, basil, nutmeg, a few drops of Tabasco sauce and extra salt and pepper, if necessary.

Serve hot.

Serves 6.

HINT
• 200 g (250 ml) uncooked rice makes about 500 ml cooked rice.

Chicken paella

Mock bobotie

Mock bobotie

Bobotie is her family's favourite dish, writes Mrs Marlene Jooste of Fauna, Bloemfontein. This bobotie recipe contains no meat, but tastes delicious.

1 kg (6 x 250 ml) cooked rice
100 g seedless raisins
2 slices white bread (crusts removed), soaked in milk and mashed
1 large onion, finely chopped
15 ml curry powder
15 ml turmeric
30 ml sugar
5 ml salt
black pepper to taste
50 g soft butter
60 ml chutney
30 ml smooth apricot jam
30 ml brown grape vinegar
30 ml tomato sauce
250 ml milk
2 extra-large eggs
2 bay leaves

Preheat the oven to 180 °C (350 °F). Spray a 26 x 22-cm oven dish with non-stick spray.

Blend all the ingredients for the bobotie, except the milk, eggs and bay leaves, in a large mixing bowl and turn into the prepared oven dish.

Beat the milk and eggs together and pour over. Place the bay leaves on top and bake for 30-40 minutes or till the dish is baked through and set.

Serve with banana slices, a salad and chutney.

Serves 6-8.

Rice surprise

This dish was devised in a time of need when there was hardly any meat in the fridge and the end of the month was still a long way off, writes Mrs Ansie Matthee of Witbank. An added advantage of this recipe is that you can use any meat, she says. For her first attempt she used a piece of sausage and the next time round she made it with two hamburger patties and a little mince. There are an endless number of variations. You can add any vegetables, like mushrooms, green peppers, peas and beans.

500 g (or less) mince
oil
2 onions, sliced
3 cloves garlic, crushed
2 medium-sized ripe tomatoes, skinned and diced
half of a can (65 g) tomato paste, blended with a little water
Worcester sauce to taste
5 ml basil
2 ml origanum
500-700 ml cooked rice

Brown small quantities of the mince at a time in heated oil in a large frying pan. Remove from the pan and set aside.

Sauté the onion and garlic in the same pan till soft. Reduce the heat and add the meat, tomato, tomato paste and all the seasonings. Simmer for a few minutes and finally add the rice. Mix and heat till warmed through.

Serve with a green salad and fresh bread rolls, if preferred.

Serves 4-6.

Rice surprise

Rice with Vienna sausages

Rice with Vienna sausages

Mrs Ansie Haarhoff of Parys devised this recipe one day when she ran out of meat. If you wish, use pork or beef sausages instead of the Vienna sausages.

1 large onion, finely chopped
oil
100 g (125 ml) rice
1 chicken stock cube
400 ml hot water
8 Vienna sausages, cut into pieces
25 ml tomato sauce
25 ml Worcester sauce
25 ml chutney
salt and pepper to taste
1 can (410 g) beans in tomato sauce

Sauté the onion in a little oil till soft. Add the rice and stir-fry till the rice has browned slightly.

Dissolve the chicken stock cube in the hot water and pour over the rice mixture in the pan. Cover and heat for about 10 minutes. Add the Vienna sausages and the seasoning and simmer till the rice is soft. Add a little extra water, if necessary. Add the beans in tomato sauce to the rice and Vienna mixture, mix and heat till warmed through.

Serve with a salad.

Serves 4.

Russian risotto

Russian risotto

Julie Saunders of Pietermaritzburg uses yellow rice when making this dish. Instead of Russian sausages, use Vienna sausages or even cooked boerewors.

2 onions, sliced
3 cloves garlic, crushed
oil
1 large green pepper, seeded and sliced
4 stalks celery, sliced into rings
2 large carrots, scraped and sliced into thin rings or strips
3-4 Russian sausages, sliced
4 x 250 ml cooked white or yellow rice
salt and pepper to taste

Sauté the onion and garlic in a little oil till soft. Add the green pepper, celery and carrot and stir-fry for 5 minutes or till the vegetables are just soft but still slightly crisp. Remove from the pan and fry the Russian sausages in the pan till done, adding more oil if necessary.

Add the cooked rice and vegetable mixture. Mix everything together and season with salt and pepper to taste. Heat till warmed through and serve immediately.

Serves 4.

Rice dish

Try using fish or Vienna sausages instead of bully beef. Pour over a generous quantity of white sauce to make the dish even more substantial. This is a firm family favourite, writes Betty Mathews of Heuwelsig, Bloemfontein.

3 x 250 ml cooked rice
1 onion, sliced into rings
1 green pepper, diced
1 stalk celery, chopped
oil
1 can (300 g) bully beef, diced
2 hard-boiled eggs, shelled and sliced
500 ml medium thick white sauce
50 g (125 ml) Cheddar cheese, grated

Preheat the oven to 180 °C (350 °F). Grease an ovenproof dish with margarine.

Spoon half the rice into the ovenproof dish.

Sauté the onion, green pepper and celery in a little oil till soft. Spoon half the mixture on top of the rice and sprinkle with half the diced bully beef and arrange the hard-boiled egg slices on top. Pour over a layer of white sauce. Repeat the layers, ending with a layer of white sauce. Sprinkle with the Cheddar cheese. Bake for about 20 minutes or till the dish is warmed through and the cheese has melted.

Serves 4.

Rice dish

Rice and eggs

Rice and eggs

She devised this dish to use up leftover cooked rice and it turned out to be a great success, writes Jeanette Elske of Sasolburg. The sauce can be made in the microwave oven.

2 onions, finely chopped
1 clove garlic, crushed
oil
625 ml cooked rice
50 ml finely chopped parsley
15 ml butter or margarine
300 ml milk
25 ml cornflour
5 ml mustard powder
2 ml paprika
salt and freshly ground black pepper
100 g (250 ml) Cheddar cheese, grated
4 hard-boiled eggs, shelled and halved

Sauté the onion and garlic in a little oil till soft. Add the cooked rice and parsley and stir-fry for about 1 minute longer. Transfer to a serving dish.

Place the butter and milk in a glass bowl and microwave for 3-4 minutes on 100% power. Stir after 1 minute.

Blend the cornflour, mustard powder and paprika with a little water to form a smooth paste. Add to the milk. Season to taste with salt and freshly ground black pepper. Microwave for about 5 minutes on 100% power or till the sauce comes to the boil and thickens. Stir at 1-minute intervals. Add three quarters of the Cheddar cheese and stir till melted.

Arrange the eggs on top of the rice mixture. Pour over the sauce and sprinkle the remaining cheese on top. Microwave for another 1-2 minutes or till the cheese has just melted.

Serves 4.

Egg and rice bake

 Light meals 

Light meals

Egg and rice bake

Onion and tomato mix is added to rice and then an egg for each person is broken onto the bed of rice. Use a large pan with ovenproof handles, otherwise everything has to be transferred to an ovenproof dish. If you like hot food, sprinkle the eggs with a little chilli powder, writes Beauty Mthethwa of Shongwe Mission.

2 onions, finely chopped
1 green chilli, seeded and finely chopped (optional)
1 red pepper, seeded and diced
oil
4 tomatoes, skinned and finely chopped
salt and freshly ground black pepper
Italian herbs
origanum
pinch sugar
750 ml or more cooked rice
4 eggs

Preheat the oven to 180 °C (350 °F).

Sauté the onion, chilli and red pepper in a little oil in a large pan till soft. Add the tomatoes and season to taste with salt, freshly ground black pepper and the other seasonings. Add a pinch of sugar if necessary. Simmer till the tomatoes are slightly soft. Add the rice and mix lightly.

Turn the rice mixture into a flat ovenproof dish if the pan can't be used in the oven. Make four hollows in the rice mixture and break an egg into each hollow. Bake for about 20 minutes or till the eggs are done.

Serves 4.

Curry and cabbage omelette

Curry and cabbage omelette

A deliciously filling omelette, made with samp and cabbage. You can prepare it on top of the stove in a pan or turn the mixture into an ovenproof dish and bake it in the oven till set. Miriam Koaho of Virginia serves the omelette with freshly baked bread and a salad.

200 g (250 ml) samp
6 extra-large eggs, beaten
125 ml sour milk or natural yoghurt
1 onion, finely chopped
oil
15 ml mild curry powder
4 x 250 ml cabbage, shredded
2-3 large, ripe tomatoes, skinned and finely chopped
salt and pepper to taste
pinch sugar
1 tomato, sliced into rings
extra sour milk or natural yoghurt (optional)

Preheat the oven to 180 °C (350 °F).

Cover the samp with cold water and soak overnight. Pour off the water, cover with fresh water and boil till soft. Season with salt at the end of the cooking time. Drain and mash lightly with a potato masher. Set aside.

Beat the eggs and sour milk together and set aside.

Sauté the onion in a little oil till soft. Add the curry powder and stir-fry for 1 minute. Add the cabbage and stir-fry till tender but still crisp. Add the tomato and samp, mix and season well with salt and pepper and a pinch of sugar if necessary. Simmer till the tomato is soft. Turn into an ovenproof dish if baking the dish in the oven.

Pour over the egg mixture, mix lightly and top with the tomato slices. Bake for 10-15 minutes or till the egg mixture has set and is done. (Do not overbake or the dish will dry out.) Slice and serve with sour milk or natural yoghurt, if preferred.

Serves 6.

Eggs with baked beans

Eggs with baked beans and mashed potato make a filling meal. Serve with a slice of fried tomato to complete the meal. She often makes this dish for supper, writes Mrs Riekie Espach of Sebasa.

3-4 medium-sized potatoes
50 ml milk
salt and pepper to taste
pinch nutmeg
oil
1 onion, sliced
2 cloves garlic, crushed
1 can (410 g) baked beans in tomato sauce
pinch thyme
25 ml brown vinegar
10 ml white sugar
few drops Worcester sauce
4 eggs
1 tomato, sliced

Boil the potatoes in their jackets in salted water till done. Remove the skins and mash with a potato masher while hot. Add the milk and season to taste with salt and pepper and a pinch of nutmeg.

Heat a little oil in a pan with a lid. Sauté the onion and garlic till soft. Add the beans in tomato sauce. Season with thyme, brown vinegar, sugar, Worcester sauce and salt and pepper to taste. Simmer till the mixture has formed a thick sauce.

Make four hollows in the sauce and break the eggs into these. Season lightly with salt and pepper, cover and heat till the eggs are done. (Alternatively, prepare the eggs separately.)

Fry the tomato slices in a little oil till lightly browned.

Serve the mashed potato, sauce, eggs and the tomato slices together.

Serves 4.

Eggs with baked beans

Egg in tomato sauce

Pan omelette

Egg in tomato sauce

Eggs are still the cheapest source of protein. Served with toast and salad, eggs make a deliciously light nourishing meal. Elizabeth Masaballa of Mokodumela sometimes makes a cheese sauce to go with this dish, but it tastes just as good without the sauce.

2 onions, sliced
oil
4-5 ripe tomatoes, skinned and finely chopped
15 ml white sugar
5 ml salt
freshly ground black pepper to taste
4 eggs
4 slices toast

Sauté the onion in a little heated oil till soft in a covered pan. Add the tomatoes and stir-fry for about 1 minute. Reduce the heat, season with sugar, salt and black pepper, and simmer till a thick sauce forms.

Make four hollows in the sauce and break the eggs into these. Cover and heat slowly till the eggs are done. Serve with the toast.

Alternatively, the eggs can be poached separately and served with the sauce and toast.

Serves 4.

Pan omelette

Rieki Espach of Tzaneen serves this dish as a light lunch or for breakfast.

500 g potatoes, peeled and diced
1 small onion, coarsely chopped
½ small green pepper, diced
oil
1 can (300 g) bully beef, diced
4 eggs
5 ml mustard powder
5 ml basil
salt and pepper to taste
Cheddar cheese for sprinkling on top (optional)

Boil the diced potato in water till soft. Drain. In a large pan, sauté the onion and green pepper in a little heated oil till soft. Add the potatoes and bully beef and stir-fry for about 2 minutes. Spread the mixture evenly in the pan.

Beat the eggs and seasonings together and pour over the mixture in the pan. Sprinkle with a little grated cheese, if preferred. Cover, reduce the heat and heat till the egg mixture has set. Lift the sides of the omelette to allow the uncooked egg to run underneath and cook.

Serve with a salad.

Serves 3.

Special macaroni and eggs

Macaroni makes scrambled eggs go much further, providing a filling meal for a group of people, writes Mrs Miriam Swanepoel of Windhoek, who is in the process of compiling a recipe book of all her family's favourite recipes.

Special macaroni and eggs

125 g elbow macaroni
4 rashers bacon, cut into smaller pieces
1 onion, finely chopped
2 cloves garlic, crushed
8 eggs, beaten
50 -100 g (125-250 ml) Cheddar cheese, grated
125 ml milk
salt and black pepper to taste
chopped parsley (optional)

Boil the macaroni in rapidly boiling salted water till just soft. Drain and set aside.

Fry the bacon in a large frying pan till slightly crisp. Add the onion and garlic and sauté in the pan fat till just soft. Add the eggs and stir till cooked but not dry – the mixture should resemble scrambled eggs.

Add the Cheddar cheese, milk and macaroni, mix well and cook slowly till heated through and the cheese has just melted. Season to taste with salt and black pepper and sprinkle with a little chopped parsley, if preferred.

Serve immediately with a salad.

Serves 6.

Oven-baked rice and curried eggs

Bettie van Tonder of Monte Vista spoons rice into the bottom of an ovenproof dish, arranges hard-boiled eggs on top and covers the dish with a curry and apple sauce.

1 small apple, peeled and diced
1 onion, sliced
15 ml butter
10 ml cake flour
15 ml curry powder
250 ml milk
30 ml chutney
salt and pepper to taste
250 ml cooked rice
1 egg, whisked
½ small onion, finely chopped
4 hard-boiled eggs, shelled and quartered
breadcrumbs and chopped parsley for sprinkling on top (optional)

Preheat the oven to 180 °C (350 °F). Grease an ovenproof dish with margarine.

Oven-baked rice and curried eggs

Tomato and samp dish

Sauté the apple and onion in the butter till soft. Stir in the cake flour and curry powder and mix well. Slowly add the milk and stir continuously. Heat till the mixture comes to the boil and thickens. Season with chutney and salt and pepper to taste.

Mix the rice with the egg and onion. Spoon into the bottom of the prepared oven dish. Arrange the hard-boiled eggs on top and pour over the curry sauce. Sprinkle with breadcrumbs if preferred and bake for about 30 minutes till heated through.

Serve with a salad.

Serves 3-4.

Tomato and samp dish

Samp needn't be only a side dish – it can become a tasty light meal. If preferred, serve this dish with meat or sausage. Mrs S Muhlner of Villieria, Pretoria sent us the recipe.

500 ml samp, soaked overnight
salt
butter or margarine
milk (optional)
1 onion, finely chopped
oil
3 tomatoes, skinned and finely chopped
freshly ground black pepper to taste
60 g (150 ml) Cheddar cheese, grated

Pour off the soaking water and cover the samp with fresh cold water. Bring to the boil and simmer till soft. Season with salt towards the end of the cooking time. Drain and mash slightly with a potato masher. Add a knob of butter and a little milk, if preferred.

Sauté the onion in a little oil till soft. Add the tomato and simmer till a sauce is formed. Season with salt and pepper and add the samp. Mix lightly, add half the cheese and mix. Sprinkle with the remaining cheese.

Serves 3-4.

Cheesy beans

Mrs F Roberts of Hennenman adds extra flavour to baked beans by stirring in some Cheddar cheese. It takes just seconds to make this tasty dish.

1 onion, finely chopped
2 cloves garlic, crushed
oil
2 tomatoes, skinned and finely chopped
2 cans (410 g) baked beans in tomato sauce
100 g (250 ml) Cheddar cheese, grated
30 ml finely chopped parsley

Sauté the onion and garlic in a little oil till soft. Add the tomato and simmer till the tomato is soft. Add the baked beans and heat till warmed through.

Remove from the heat and add the cheese. Stir till the cheese has melted.

Sprinkle with parsley and serve with rice.

Serves 2-3.

Potato pan-fry

Mrs M Armstrong of Tamboerskloof arranges layers of cooked potato and frankfurters in a dish, adds a sprinkling of cheese and then bakes the dish for about 30 minutes in a moderate oven.

We prepared the dish in a pan.

6 frankfurters, sliced
oil
6 potatoes, boiled, peeled and diced
100 g Cheddar cheese, diced

Fry the sliced frankfurters in a little oil till done. Remove from the pan and drain on paper towelling. Fry the potato slices in the same pan till slightly crisp and drain on paper towelling.

Arrange layers of potato and sausage in a dish or directly on each person's plate, sprinkle with the diced Cheddar cheese and heat till the cheese just begins to melt and the dish is heated through. (It takes about 1 minute in the microwave oven on 100% power.)

Serve with a salad.

Serves 4-6.

Red lentil curry

Serve this lentil curry with rice. Faiza Davids of Mitchell's Plain sent us the recipe.

200 g (250 ml) red lentils, rinsed
1 onion, finely chopped
2 cloves garlic, crushed
oil
2 ml cayenne pepper
5 ml ground cumin (jeera)
5 ml turmeric
1 large ripe tomato, skinned and diced
salt to taste
4 hard-boiled eggs, shelled and quartered or sliced

Boil the lentils in salted water till soft. Drain and set aside.

Sauté the onion and garlic in a little oil till soft. Add the cayenne pepper, cumin, and turmeric and stir-fry for another minute. Add the tomato, reduce the heat and simmer for a few minutes. Add the lentils and mix well. Season with salt. Heat till warm.

Serve the eggs with the lentils.

Serves 3-4.

Lentil bobotie

This bobotie recipe, sent in by Mrs Sadie Stegmann of Mowbray, contains no meat but the lentils provide more than enough protein. Served with rice, chutney, coconut and chopped tomato and onion sambal it makes for a fully balanced meal.

LENTIL MIXTURE
200 g (250 ml) uncooked brown lentils, sorted and rinsed
salt to taste
3 slices brown bread, crusts removed
150 ml milk or water
2 onions, sliced
2 cloves garlic, crushed
oil
15 ml mild curry powder
5 ml turmeric
5 ml ground coriander
3 ml ground cumin (jeera)
45 ml white grape vinegar
60 ml chutney

Cheesy beans

Potato pan-fry

Red lentil curry

Lentil bobotie

Mealie meal burgers

Bread stir-fry

15 ml Worcester sauce
7 ml salt
freshly ground black pepper to taste
60 ml seedless raisins

TOPPING
1 egg
60 ml milk
1 banana, halved (optional)
1 bay leaf (optional)

Preheat the oven to 180 °C (350 °F). Spray a 19-cm ovenproof dish with non-stick spray.

Boil the lentils in sufficient salted water till soft. Drain well and turn into a large mixing bowl.

Soak the brown bread in the milk or water. Mash and add it to the lentils.

Sauté the onion and garlic in the oil till soft. Add the curry powder, turmeric, coriander and cumin and stir-fry for about 1 minute. Add the remaining seasonings and the raisins and blend well. Add to the lentil mixture.

Turn the mixture into the prepared oven dish.

Prepare the topping: Beat the egg and milk together, pour over the lentil mixture. Make holes in the lentil mixture with a fork to allow the egg mixture to spread evenly. Arrange the banana halves and bay leaf on top, if preferred. Bake for 30-40 minutes or till the milk mixture has set.

Serves 4.

HINTS
- Remember to sort the lentils beforehand because they often contain tiny stones which look exactly like lentils. Rinse the lentils under cold running water. You needn't soak the lentils beforehand as they do not take that long to cook.
- Lentils are one of the few VAT-free products, and are an excellent substitute for meat. Alternatively, use them to supplement meat.

Mealie meal burgers

Make these mealie meal burgers instead of hamburger rolls and serve with egg, tomato and onion for a deliciously light yet nourishing meal. They are also very good served for breakfast, writes Mrs Avril Strydom of Stilfontein.

60 g (125 ml) cake flour
60 g (125 ml) mealie meal
2 ml salt
5 ml baking powder
250 ml milk
oil
about 6 slices tomato, lightly fried in oil, if preferred
about 6 fried eggs
2 onions, sliced and sautéed in a little oil till soft

Combine the cake flour, mealie meal, salt and baking powder in a mixing bowl. Add the milk and blend to form a smooth batter. (Stir with a wire beater.) Leave the batter to rest for a few minutes.

Brush a pan with a little oil before heating it. Spoon tablespoonfuls of the batter into the pan and fry till brown underneath. (Air bubbles will begin to form on top.) Turn the patties over with an egg slice and fry till brown on the other side.

Top each mealie meal burger with a slice of tomato and a fried egg. Sprinkle with a little sautéed onion and place another mealiemeal burger on top.

Serve with a salad, if preferred.

Makes about 6 mealie meal burgers.

Bread stir-fry

Dorothy Loggenberg of Lynnwoodrif, in Pretoria, writes that she made this dish in desperation one evening when she unexpectedly had to prepare supper.

250 g chopped bacon
500 ml bread, diced or crumbled
1 onion, sliced into rings or finely chopped
2 cloves garlic, crushed
1 egg, whisked (optional)
pepper to taste
oil for frying

Mix all the ingredients except the oil and stir-fry in a little oil over medium heat till the bacon is done and the bread is golden brown and crisp.

Serve with a green salad and salad dressing.

Serves 3-4.

Tuna snack

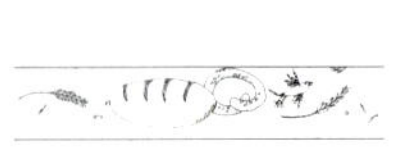

Bread as meals and snacks

Tuna snack

Delicious as a light meal or a snack. Zerilda du Toit of Empangeni likes to serve this delicious tuna dish for lunch on Saturdays.

6 slices white bread, crusts removed
butter or margarine
Old Cape mustard
1 onion, finely chopped
2 cloves garlic, crushed
oil
2 cans (200 g each) shredded tuna, drained
75 ml finely chopped parsley
150 g (375 ml) Cheddar cheese, grated
1 large tomato, skinned and sliced
salt and pepper to taste
250 ml milk
2 eggs
5 ml paprika

Preheat the oven to 180 °C (350 °F).

Butter the slices of bread on both sides. Spread one side of each slice of bread with a little mustard. (If you do not have Old Cape mustard, blend a little mustard powder with the butter before buttering the bread – 5 ml per 100 ml butter should be enough.) Arrange the bread in a 30 x 21 x 5-cm ovenproof dish.

Sauté the onion and garlic in a little oil till soft. Add the tuna and parsley. Spoon onto the bread. Sprinkle with the cheese and decorate with the tomato slices. Season well with salt and pepper.

Beat the milk, eggs and paprika together and pour over the tuna mixture. Bake for 30 minutes or till the egg mixture has set.

Serve hot.

Serves 6.

HINT

- To make the dish even more economical, use only 100 g (250 ml) cheese.

Eggs in a blanket

This recipe and the one for bacon sandwiches (see p. 58) make the ideal light meal to serve for one or two people, writes Mrs I A du Plessis of Parow. Serve as a light lunch or supper or even for breakfast.

2 hard-boiled eggs, shelled and sliced into thin rings
2 slices toast, buttered on one side
salt
75 g (180 ml) Tusser's or Cheddar cheese, grated
1 egg, lightly beaten
2 ml mustard powder
pepper to taste
30 ml chopped parsley or fresh chives (optional)

Arrange the sliced eggs on the buttered sides of the slices of toast. Season lightly with salt.

Mix the remaining ingredients together, divide in half and spoon onto each slice of toast. Place under the oven grill or in the microwave oven till the cheese has just melted.

Serve hot.

Serves 2.

Eggs in a blanket

Pan bread with soya mince

Pan bread with soya mince

Served with hot pan bread and a sprinkling of cheese, you would hardly believe you were eating soya. The bread is also delicious with soup, writes Renée Franco of Gardens. Alternatively, the soya mince may be served with yellow rice and a salad.

PAN BREAD

500 g (880 ml) self-raising flour
5 ml salt
20 ml sugar
7 ml instant yeast (half a 10 g packet)
30 ml oil
300 ml lukewarm water

SOYA MINCE

1 onion, finely chopped
5 large cloves garlic, crushed
1 green pepper, seeded and diced
oil
1 packet (120 g) dry soya mince (e.g. savoury from Toppers)
500 ml boiling water
half a 65-g can tomato paste
12,5 ml sugar
salt and freshly ground black pepper to taste
grated Cheddar cheese

Mix the self-raising flour, salt and sugar and sprinkle with the instant yeast.

Pour over the oil and the lukewarm water. Mix to form a stiff dough and knead till the dough is smooth and elastic and no longer clings to your hands. Cover with plastic wrap and rest for 10 minutes. Punch down and divide into 12 uniform balls. Leave to rise till double in bulk. Flatten the balls slightly and fry in a heated pan brushed with a little oil. Fry till brown on both sides and cooked inside.

Sauté the onion, garlic and green pepper in oil till soft.

Add the soya mince and enough boiling water to cook the soya till soft.

Add the remaining ingredients and simmer till done. Serve with the pan bread and a sprinkling of cheese.

Serves 8-10.

Sandwich bake

Quick and easy to prepare. This recipe was sent in by Miss S Zandberg of Carters Glen, Kimberley.

margarine for spreading on the bread
5 ml French mustard (optional)
8 slices white bread, crusts removed
1 tomato, thinly sliced
100 g (250 ml) Cheddar cheese, grated
salt and freshly ground black pepper
3 eggs, beaten
300 ml milk
2 ml mustard powder
pinch cayenne pepper

Preheat the oven to 180 °C (350 °F). Grease a 26 x 22-cm ovenproof dish with margarine.

Blend the margarine and mustard together. Spread one side of each slice of bread with the margarine mixture. Arrange slices of tomato on the spread sides of the bread slices and sprinkle with a little cheese. Season with salt and black pepper and cover with the remaining four slices of bread. Cut each sandwich into quarters and arrange in the prepared dish. Sprinkle the remaining cheese on top.

Beat the eggs and milk together and season with the mustard powder and cayenne pepper, and salt and pepper to taste. Pour the mixture over the sandwiches and bake for 45 minutes or till the egg mixture is cooked through and has set.

Serve immediately.

Serves 4.

Bacon sandwiches

Serve these sandwiches plain or toasted. You can even dip them in an egg and milk mixture and fry them in oil till golden brown. This recipe was sent in by Mrs I A du Plessis of Parow.

2 hard-boiled eggs, shelled and mashed
50 ml mayonnaise
4 rashers cooked bacon, finely chopped
salt and pepper to taste
6 slices white bread, buttered

Sandwich bake

Bacon sandwiches

Pizza bites

Mix the mashed eggs, mayonnaise and bacon together and season to taste with salt and pepper. Make sandwiches with the mixture.

Serve plain or toasted, or dip each sandwich in an egg and milk mixture – 1 egg for every 100 ml milk – and fry in oil till golden brown.

Serve immediately.

Serves 2.

Pizza bites

These pizza bites make a delicious light meal and are great with a braai, writes Miss Marina Smalberger of Stellenbosch.

9 slices white bread (crusts removed), halved
1-2 tomatoes, skinned and diced
4 rashers bacon, diced
100 g (250 ml) Cheddar cheese, grated
2-3 extra-large eggs, beaten
salt and black pepper to taste

Preheat the oven to 180 °C (350 °F). Arrange the halved bread slices on a baking sheet lined with tin foil.

Blend the tomato, bacon, cheese and eggs and season well with salt and black pepper. Spoon a little of the mixture on each slice of bread, spreading it evenly. Bake for about 20 minutes till the cheese has melted and the bacon is slightly crisp and cooked.

Serve hot or cold.

Serves 6 for a light meal.

VARIATION

- Toast one side of each slice of bread. Fry the bacon beforehand and mix with the remaining ingredients. Use only 1-2 eggs, otherwise the mixture runs down the sides. Spread the mixture on the untoasted side of the bread slices. Toast under the oven grill till the cheese just melts.

Garlic rolls

Stale bread rolls need not end up in the dog's bowl, writes Luitjé Mulder of Thabazimbi.

Serve each person an individual roll with garlic butter or any other spread.

110 g soft butter
salt and pepper
15 ml chopped parsley
3 large cloves garlic, crushed
6 long, stale bread rolls

Blend the butter, salt and pepper, parsley and garlic.

Slice the bread rolls, but not all the way through (as you would slice a French loaf). Spread both sides of each slice generously with the butter mixture and wrap individually in tin foil.

Heat over the coals or in a hot oven at 180 °C (350 °F) till the butter has melted and the rolls are crisp. Serve the bread rolls with braaivleis.

Serves 6.

Garlic rolls

Mealie meal bites

For a delicious snack, cut cold stiff mealie meal porridge into squares and fry till brown. Serve as is for a snack or with tomato sauce as a side dish with meat or sausage.

200 g (350 ml) mealie meal
2 ml salt
450 ml water
little cayenne pepper (optional)
2 eggs, whisked
60 g (250 ml) fresh breadcrumbs
oil for frying

Spray a medium-sized baking tray with non-stick spray.

Blend the mealie meal and salt with a little water to form a paste. Bring the remaining water to the boil and add the mealie meal paste, stirring continuously till the mixture comes to the boil. Simmer for about 20 minutes till the porridge is done. Season with a little cayenne pepper, if preferred. Turn the mixture into the prepared baking tray, pressing it evenly into the tray. Cool.

Cut the porridge into squares, dip in the whisked egg and roll in the breadcrumbs. Fry in heated oil till brown.

Serve with tomato sauce, if preferred.

Makes 30 squares.

Mealie meal bites

Bean and potato patties

Bean and potato patties

Mrs Ursula Comfort of East London packs these patties into the children's lunch boxes or serves them as a snack or an accompaniment for a light meal.

3 large potatoes, peeled and coarsely grated
1 large onion, finely chopped and lightly sautéed
1 can (410 g) chilli beans
2 eggs, whisked
125 g (225 ml) cake flour
5 ml baking powder
5 ml mixed herbs
5 ml sugar
salt and pepper to taste
oil for frying

Pat the potatoes dry and mix with all the remaining ingredients, except the oil. Heat the oil in a pan and drop spoonfuls of the mixture into the oil. Fry till the patties are golden brown and cooked inside.

Makes about 30 potato patties.

Vegetable patties

Savoury vegetables

Vegetable patties

Serve these delicious vegetable patties with tomato sauce. They have a delicious curry flavour and are delicious served with a salad. The recipe was sent in by Florinah Seapa of Kimberley.

50 ml margarine
70 g (125 ml) cake flour
375 ml milk
boiling water
250 ml frozen vegetables
500 ml cooked rice
5 hard-boiled eggs, shelled and finely chopped
25 ml finely chopped parsley
5 ml curry powder
salt and pepper to taste
1 egg, whisked
breadcrumbs for rolling in
oil for deep-frying

Make a white sauce: Melt the margarine in a large saucepan. Add the cake flour and stir well. Cook for 1 minute. Heat the milk slightly and add small quantities at a time to the cake flour mixture in the saucepan. Stir well. Heat till the mixture comes to the boil and thickens. Remove from the heat.

Pour boiling water over the frozen vegetables, leave for 5 minutes and drain well. Add to the white sauce, along with the remaining ingredients, except the crumbs and oil. Shape the mixture, which is fairly soft, into hamburger patties and roll in the crumbs. Place on a baking sheet and chill for 30 minutes. Deep-fry in oil till golden brown. Drain on paper towelling and serve with a salad and tomato sauce.

Makes 15 patties.

Cabbage and bully beef

Cabbage stir-fry with bacon

Cabbage and bully beef

Most kitchen cupboards are stocked with a standby can of bully beef. Christel Burckhardt of Southdale writes that this dish, served with a slice of bread or a bread roll, makes a delicious meal.

2 onions, sliced
3 cloves garlic, crushed
oil
700 g cabbage, shredded finely
5 ml caraway seeds
1 can (300 g) bully beef, diced
5 potatoes, peeled and diced
250 ml chicken stock
salt and pepper
pinch nutmeg

Sauté the onion and garlic in a little oil till soft. Add the cabbage and caraway seeds and stir-fry till glossy. Remove from the pan and set aside.

Stir-fry the diced bully beef in the oil in the pan till brown and remove from the pan (add more oil if necessary).

Fry the diced potato lightly, add the chicken stock, cover and simmer till soft.

Add the cabbage mixture and the bully beef. Mix and season to taste with salt and pepper and a pinch of nutmeg. Stir-fry till heated through.

Serve hot.

Serves 6.

Cabbage stir-fry with bacon

Bacon imparts a wonderful flavour to ordinary vegetables like cabbage, carrots and potatoes. She concocted this dish one day when she was running short of vegetables, writes Mrs Mary Störm of Riversdal.

125 g bacon, cut into pieces
1 onion, coarsely chopped
oil
4 potatoes, peeled and diced
2 carrots, scraped and diced or thinly sliced
½ head cabbage, shredded
water or chicken stock
nutmeg
salt and black pepper to taste
parsley if preferred

Fry the bacon till done. Remove from the pan. Add the onion and sauté in the pan fat till soft. Add oil if necessary. Stir-fry the potato, carrot and cabbage in the oil in the pan till glossy. Add a little water or chicken stock and simmer till the vegetables are just soft but still slightly crisp. Season with a pinch of nutmeg and salt and black pepper to taste. Add bacon. Sprinkle with a little parsley if preferred.

Serve with rice.

Serves 4.

Cabbage with salami

Only a few pieces of salami are enough to impart a delicious flavour to the cabbage. Alet van Dyk of Kuils River often serves this as a light supper dish.

1 small cabbage, thinly shredded
oil
4 cooked potatoes, cut into pieces
125 g salami, sliced and quartered
juice of 1 lemon
salt and pepper to taste
25 ml butter or margarine
25 ml cake flour
250 ml milk
5 ml mustard powder
little grated Cheddar cheese

Preheat the oven to 180 °C (350 °F).

Sauté the cabbage in a little oil till just soft. Add the potato pieces and salami and mix. Season with lemon juice, salt and pepper to taste. Spoon the mixture into an ovenproof dish.

Cabbage with salami

Melt the butter and stir in the cake flour. Slowly stir in the milk till smooth and heat till the mixture comes to the boil and thickens. Stir continuously. Season with mustard powder, and salt and pepper to taste. Add a little Cheddar cheese. Pour the white sauce over the cabbage mixture, sprinkle with a little Cheddar cheese, if preferred, and place in a heated oven till the cheese has just melted and the dish is warmed through.

Serve with a salad, if preferred.

Serves 4.

Bean and cabbage curry

Miss T L Seeko of Katlehong serves porridge or rice with this cabbage dish.

oil
1 green pepper, diced or cut into strips
30 ml mild curry powder
5 ml ground coriander
5 ml ground cumin (jeera)
1 bunch carrots, scraped and sliced into thin rings
1 medium-sized cabbage, about 1,6 kg, thinly shredded
1 beef stock cube
1 can (410 g) baked beans in tomato sauce
black pepper to taste

Bean and cabbage curry

Heat the oil in a large pan and sauté the green pepper till soft. Add the curry powder, coriander and cumin and lightly stir-fry. Add the carrots and shredded cabbage and stir-fry till the vegetables are soft but still slightly crisp. Crumble the beef stock cube and stir into the mixture. Add the baked beans and mix. Heat till the dish is warmed through and season to taste with black pepper.

Serve with rice or porridge.

Serves 4-6.

Curried cabbage with eggs

Curried cabbage with eggs

Curried cabbage is delicious, and if served with eggs it makes a quick and easy meal. Ideal for when you're running low on ingredients, writes Mr D L Mostert of Rustenburg.

1 onion, sliced
1 clove garlic, crushed
oil
15 ml curry powder
3 ml ground ginger
10 ml ground coriander
10 ml mixed herbs
500 g (half a medium-sized) cabbage, finely shredded
20 ml Worcester sauce
30 ml chutney
4-6 eggs
salt and pepper

Sauté the onion and garlic in a little oil till soft. Add the seasonings, except the Worcester sauce and chutney and stir-fry for about 1 minute. Add the finely shredded cabbage and stir-fry gently. Add a little water and simmer till the cabbage is done but still crisp. Season with Worcester sauce and chutney.

Make hollows in the cabbage mixture and break the eggs into the hollows. Cover the pan and reduce the heat. Heat till the eggs are done. Season to taste with salt and pepper and serve with rice or mashed potato.

Serves 4-6.

Cabbage stir-fry with Russians

Cabbage lasagne

Cabbage stir-fry with Russians

Cabbage and Russian sausages topped with a piquant sweet-and-sour sauce. The recipe was sent in by Josie Olivier of Bloemfontein.

1 onion, sliced
oil
4 carrots, scraped and cut into julienne strips
350 g head of cabbage, shredded
2 green apples, skinned, cored and thinly sliced
4-6 Russian sausages, sliced
salt and black pepper to taste

SAUCE
5 ml mustard powder
2-5 ml sugar (or to taste)
60 ml grape vinegar

Sauté the onion in a little oil in a large pan till soft. Add the carrot and stir-fry till glazed. Add the cabbage and apple and stir-fry till just tender. Remove from the pan and set aside.

Stir-fry the sausages in a little oil till just brown, spoon the vegetables in the pan and heat till warmed through. Season with salt and black pepper. Transfer to a serving dish.

Blend all the ingredients for the sauce and pour over the sausages just before serving.

Serve with rice, pasta or fresh bread rolls, if preferred.

Serves 4.

VARIATION
• Instead of Russian sausages, use 125-250 g bacon to prepare the dish.

Cabbage lasagne

Use cabbage leaves instead of lasagne sheets and an egg custard instead of a white sauce to make this dish. This makes it easier to cut the lasagne into neat squares. Brinjals can be used instead of the mince. She often used to make this dish when she lived in Australia, writes Mrs Audrey Keyser of Beaufort West.

125 g rashers bacon, cut into pieces
1 onion, sliced into rings
2 cloves garlic, crushed
oil (optional)
250 g button mushrooms, slices (optional)
500 g mince
100 ml chutney
100 ml tomato sauce
salt and black pepper to taste
6-8 large cabbage leaves, blanched
grated Cheddar cheese
4 eggs
250 ml milk
5 ml mustard powder

Preheat the oven to 180 °C (350 °F). Grease a large ovenproof dish with margarine.

Fry the bacon in a pan till done but not crisp. Add the onion and garlic and sauté till soft. Add the oil, if necessary. Add the mushrooms and stir-fry till pale brown. Remove from the pan and fry the mince in the pan till done but not brown. Add the chutney and tomato sauce and return the vegetable mixture to the pan. Season to taste with salt and black pepper and simmer till a flavoursome mince sauce is formed.

Arrange 2 cabbage leaves in the bottom of the prepared dish and cover with a layer of the mince sauce. Sprinkle with a layer of cheese. Repeat the layers, ending with a layer of cabbage leaves. Beat the eggs, milk and mustard powder together. Season to taste with salt and pepper and pour on top. Bake for about 30 minutes or till the egg mixture has set. Cover with tin foil if the cabbage leaves start to burn.

Serves 6-8.

Cabbage with mince

An economical dish, because it makes a little mince go a long way, writes Mrs Mathilda Oberholzer of Winburg, who says her mother used to prepare the dish regularly for her family.

1 medium-sized cabbage
500 g mince

60 g (180 ml) oats
2 eggs
15 ml parsley, chopped
1 ml nutmeg
salt and black pepper to taste
butter or margarine

Preheat the oven to 180 °C (350 °F). Grease a deep 24-cm ovenproof dish with margarine.

Boil the whole cabbage for 10 minutes in a saucepan half-filled with salted water. Drain the cabbage and fill the saucepan with cold water. Cool the cabbage till you're able to hold it. Cut out the stem and break off the leaves one by one.

Line the prepared dish with a double layer of the outer large leaves, stem-end facing in and with the leaves draping over the sides of the dish.

Mix the mince with the oats, eggs and seasonings. Spoon a layer of the meat mixture on top of the leaves and line with another double layer of cabbage leaves.

Spoon the remaining mince on top and line with the remaining cabbage leaves. Dot generously with butter, cover lightly with tin foil and bake the dish for about 1-1½ hours or till the mince is done.

Serve with mashed potatoes and a salad.

Serves 4-6.

West-End hit

Living on a farm means you often have to rustle up a meal when unexpected guests stay over for supper, writes Mrs G H Reyneke of Greytown. That's when this scrambled egg dish, which has been named after their farm, is a real standby.

2 carrots, scraped and grated
oil
1 small (500 g) head cabbage, shredded
45-60 ml soy sauce (optional)
250 ml cooked rice
4 eggs
30 ml milk
salt and black pepper to taste

Sauté the carrots in a little oil till just tender. Remove from the pan and set aside.

Sauté the cabbage till just tender. Return the carrots to the pan and add the soy sauce.

Also add the cooked rice and stir-fry till the rice and vegetables are heated through.

Beat the eggs and milk together. Pour the egg mixture over the cabbage mixture and mix. Stir till the eggs are just done. Season with salt and black pepper to taste.

Serve immediately.

Serves 3-4.

Cabbage stir-fry with chicken

This cabbage stir-fry dish goes a long way, writes Mrs A Dreyer of Windhoek.

500 g deboned chicken breasts, cut into thin strips
salt and black pepper to taste
oil
15 ml ground coriander
15 ml ground ginger
1 onion, sliced
2 cloves garlic, crushed
½ head cabbage (about 500 g), shredded
4-5 carrots, cut into thin strips with a vegetable peeler
50-75 ml brown sugar
50-75 ml white grape vinegar

Season the chicken with salt and black pepper and fry in a little heated oil in a large pan till golden brown.

Add half the ground coriander and ginger while frying. Remove from the pan.

Stir-fry the onion and garlic in the pan till soft. Add the remaining coriander and ginger. Add more oil if necessary.

Add the cabbage and carrot strips and stir-fry till the vegetables are just tender but still crisp. Add the brown sugar and white grape vinegar and mix. Add the chicken strips and heat till warmed through.

Serve with rice.

Serves 6-8.

Cabbage with mince

West-End hit

Cabbage stir-fry with chicken

Potato cheese pie

This pie hardly needs any preparation – the potatoes don't have to be cooked beforehand and all you really have to do is beat the milk and eggs together. "Very good," writes Mrs Helen van Deventer of Dordrecht.

3 large potatoes, skinned
100 ml finely chopped onion
salt
100 g (250 ml) Cheddar cheese, grated
25 ml chopped parsley
2 eggs
250 ml milk
2 ml paprika
2 ml mustard powder
2 ml salt
black pepper to taste

Preheat the oven to 180 °C (350 °F). Grease a 24-cm pie dish or two 15-cm pie dishes with margarine.

Grate the potatoes coarsely using a hand grater. Rinse and pat dry with paper towelling. Mix the grated potato with the chopped onion and season with a pinch of salt. Turn into the prepared pie dishes and press evenly onto the base and along sides of the dishes.

Combine the Cheddar cheese and parsley and sprinkle over the potato crust. Beat the eggs, milk and seasonings together and pour on top. Bake for about 35-40 minutes or till the potato crust is golden brown and the filling has set.

Serve with salad and cold meats for a light meal or as a quiche. Serve hot or cold.

Serves 4.

Potato cheese pie

Leftover potato pie

Leftover potato pie

Miss A Vivier of Pretoria makes hollows in leftover mashed potato which she fills with mince and egg. Top the dish with a sprinkling of cheese, if preferred.

1 packet (200 g) instant mashed potato or 1 kg leftover mashed potato
knob of butter or margarine
5 ml mustard powder
5 ml basil
about 250 ml leftover mince
3-4 eggs
grated Cheddar cheese for sprinkling on top
chopped parsley for sprinkling on top

Preheat the oven to 180 °C (350 °F). Grease an ovenproof dish with margarine.

Mix the mashed potato and butter and season with mustard powder and basil. Spoon into the prepared dish and spread evenly. Make eight hollows in the potato with the back of a spoon and spoon a little mince into 4 or 5 of the hollows. Break an egg into each of the remaining hollows. Sprinkle with a little Cheddar cheese, if preferred, and bake for about 20 minutes or till the eggs are done. Sprinkle with chopped parsley and serve with tomato sauce.

Serves 4-6.

Sausage and potato supper dish

Her husband loves Russian sausages, which explains why this is one of his favourite dishes, writes Mrs Maureen Oberholzer of Scottburgh. She stirs a can of cream of mushroom soup into the potato mixture, tops it with cheese and breadcrumbs and bakes it till the cheese has melted and the dish is lightly browned on top.

1 onion, finely chopped
2 cloves garlic, crushed
oil
3 potatoes, skinned and cubed
250 ml chicken stock
250 ml peas
250 ml whole sweetcorn
salt and pepper to taste
4 Russian sausages

Sausage and potato supper dish

Sauté the onion and garlic in a little oil till soft. Add the potato cubes and pour over the chicken stock. Cover and simmer till the potato cubes are soft. Add the peas and sweetcorn, season with salt and pepper and simmer till warm. In the meantime, fry the sausages in a little oil till brown and cooked. Slice them, if preferred. Spoon the potato mixture onto a serving platter and arrange the sausages on top. Serve with a salad and crusty bread.

Serves 4.

Curried potatoes

Mrs Joan O'Neill of Warrenton sometimes serves this dish with toast or rice. It can also be served with leftover meat or Vienna sausages. A green salad makes a good accompaniment.

Curried potatoes

2 onions, sliced
2 green apples, skinned and diced
oil
20 ml curry powder
5 ml coriander
5 ml ground cumin (jeera)
10 ml turmeric
750 ml boiling water
80 ml white sugar
70 g (125 ml) raisins (optional)
500 g whole baby potatoes or sliced medium-sized potatoes, boiled and peeled
25 ml cake flour
4 hard-boiled eggs, shelled and halved

In a large saucepan, sauté the onion and diced apple in a little oil till soft. Add all the seasonings and stir-fry for 1 minute. (Take care that the mixture does not stick to the bottom of the saucepan.)

Add the boiling water, sugar and raisins. Stir till well blended. Heat till the sauce comes to the boil. Add the potatoes and heat till the potatoes have absorbed the sauce. If necessary, thicken the sauce with cake flour blended with a little water. Serve with the eggs or add the eggs to the mixture and heat through.

Serves 4.

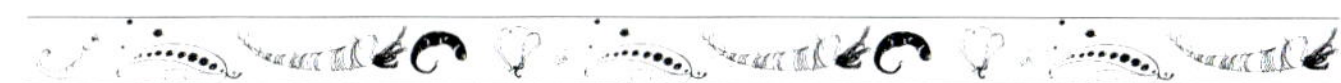

HOW TO COOK DRIED BEANS

- Ensure that the saucepan used for soaking the beans is large enough to allow for the dried beans to expand to about two-thirds their original volume.
- Do not add any bicarbonate of soda to the boiling water. This destroys the vitamins in dried beans.
- Simmer the beans slowly. If they are cooked too rapidly, the skins will burst and the beans will reduce, causing a loss in their fibre content.
- Add 15 ml oil per 250 ml dried beans during the cooking process. This prevents foam from forming.
- Add salt to the beans once they are cooked. The beans will not soften if salt is added at the beginning of the cooking process.
- Use 20 ml salt per 1 kg cooked beans (550 g uncooked).
- The cooking process is slowed down by the addition of acidic foods, so it is important to only add tomatoes, vinegar, etc. once the beans are soft.
- If using white and coloured beans in the same dish, boil the beans separately, otherwise the white beans will become tainted with the colour of the other beans.
- When using cooked beans in an oven dish, ensure that there is sufficient moisture in which to bake them, otherwise all the moisture will be extracted from the beans, leaving them tough and tasteless.
- Liquid or seasonings may be added after the beans have been defrosted.
- When cooking beans, prepare enough for more than one meal and chill or freeze the remaining beans. Pack the beans in recipe-sized bags. A little extra liquid or seasonings may be added after the beans have been defrosted.
- When a recipe calls for water as an ingredient, use the water in which the beans were cooked.

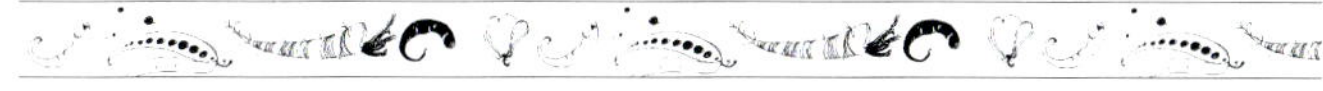

Baked potatoes

Baked potatoes

A delicious light meal of baked potato with a filling. We baked the potatoes in the microwave oven to save time.

4 uniform medium-sized potatoes
butter or margarine
salt
sour cream or natural yoghurt
Vienna sausages or leftover sausage, cut into pieces
pieces of tomato
chopped parsley for sprinkling on top

Wash the potatoes well and prick the skins all over with a fork. Line the glass platter of the microwave oven with paper towelling and arrange the potatoes in a circle on top. Microwave for 5-6 minutes on 100% power, turn and microwave for another 5-6 minutes on 100% power.

Cut a cross in each potato and press the potato at the bottom to open it up slightly. Remove a little of the potato flesh and mix with a little butter and season to taste with salt. Return to the potato hollows.

Pour a little sour cream over the potatoes, top with pieces of sausage and tomato and season to taste with salt and pepper. Microwave till the filling ingredients are just warm. Sprinkle chopped parsley over.

Serves 4.

VARIATION

- Mix grated Cheddar cheese and mustard powder with the potato flesh, spoon the mixture into the potato hollows and microwave till warm. Sprinkle chopped parsley over.

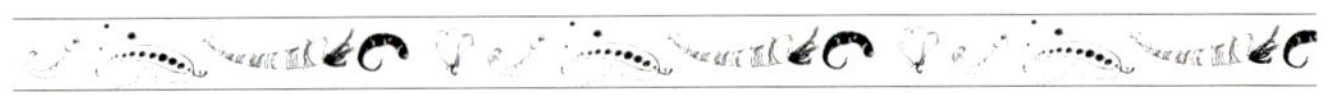

Mix leftover vegetables with a little cake flour and 1 or 2 whisked eggs and prepare flavoursome fritters by frying the mixture in shallow oil. Alternatively, liquidise leftover vegetables and use the mixture to thicken sauces. Or try marinating the vegetables in French salad dressing for a few hours and serve as a salad.

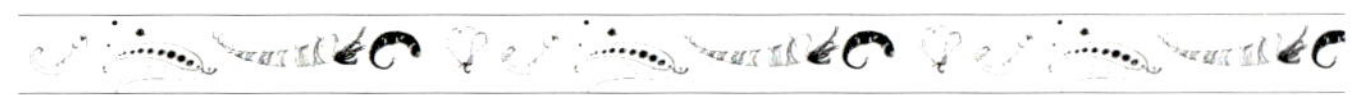

Buy fruit and vegetables that are in season as this makes good economic sense. Usually each season has its respective variety of fruit and vegetables to choose from.

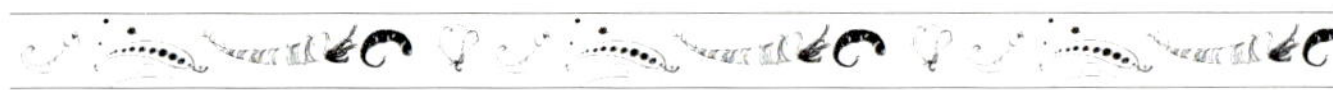

Potato dish

This delicious dish makes a filling, economical meal, say Mrs H Boogers of Piet Retief, who sometimes makes it in a potjie over glowing coals.

250 g bacon, rind removed
5 large onions, sliced
3 cloves garlic, crushed
12 large potatoes, peeled and thinly sliced
50 ml butter or margarine
5-10 ml thyme
rice spice
salt and freshly ground black pepper to taste

Preheat the oven to 180 °C (350 °F).

Fry the bacon in a potjie till done. Remove the bacon and set aside.

Sauté the onion and garlic till tender and glazed. Remove and set aside.

Arrange half the potato slices in the pot. Dot with half the butter and season to taste with all the seasonings. Top with the onion mixture and sprinkle with the bacon, reserving a few rashers for garnishing.

Top with the remaining potato slices, dot with the remaining butter and again season to taste with all the seasonings. Sprinkle with the reserved bacon, cover and bake for 1 hour or till the potato slices are done and the top is lightly crisped. Remove the lid for the last 15 minutes of the cooking time. Remember to stir the contents of the pot occasionally if the dish is cooked over the coals.

Serve with a mixed salad.

Serves 8.

Potato dish

Egg and spinach dish

Rethabile Monyau of Maseru in Lesotho often serves this dish for supper.

6 rashers bacon, cut into pieces
oil (optional)
2 onions, coarsely chopped
1 large carrot, thinly sliced
1 bunch (300 g) spinach (rinsed and hard stems removed), shredded
grated rind of lemon
salt and pepper to taste
4 soft fried eggs

Fry the bacon in a pan till done but not crisp. Add more oil to the pan if necessary and sauté the onion and carrot till soft. Add the spinach and stir-fry till soft. Season with the lemon rind and salt and pepper to taste. Transfer to a serving platter and make four hollows in the vegetable mixture. Place the eggs on top and serve with homemade tomato sauce, if preferred. Alternatively, break raw eggs into the hollows and bake the dish at 180 °C (350 °F) till the eggs are done.

Serves 4.

Vegetable macaroni

Turn frozen mixed vegetables into a filling meal by flavouring it with curry and mixing it with macaroni or other pasta. Hemlata Bagratee of Park Rynie tops the dish with grated cheese and breadcrumbs and browns it in the oven.

1 packet (500 g) macaroni or other pasta
1 onion, sliced
30 ml oil
5 ml curry powder
5 ml garam masala
5 ml ground cumin (jeera)
pinch chilli powder (optional)
1 kg mixed frozen vegetables
2 potatoes, peeled and diced (optional)
salt to taste

Cook the macaroni in rapidly boiling salted water till just soft. Drain and set aside.

In a large saucepan, sauté the onion in heated oil till just soft. Add the curry powder, garam masala, cumin and chilli powder and stir-fry for about 1 minute.

Add the vegetables and potatoes, mix, reduce the heat and simmer till the vegetables are just tender. Add a little water, if necessary. Season with salt to taste. Add the drained macaroni and mix. Heat the dish till warmed through.

Serve with grated cheese.

Serves 8.

Curried pumpkin

Serve the pumpkin with rice and a meat stew, writes Miss Sizakele Mabaso of Madadeni. The recipe also calls for chillies. Dry any leftover chillies and simply soak in water when needed again.

1 large onion, sliced
2 cloves garlic, crushed
2 pieces cinnamon
2 chillies, seeded and sliced into rings (optional)
oil
15 ml mild curry powder
5 ml ground cumin (jeera)
2 kg flat white pumpkin, peeled and sliced
salt to taste
100 ml sugar or to taste
chopped parsley

Sauté the onion, garlic, cinnamon and chilli in a little oil till the onion is soft. Add the mild curry powder and ground cumin and stir-fry for about 1 minute, taking care that the mixture does not burn.

Add the pumpkin slices and a little water. Season with salt and simmer till the pumpkin is soft, but not mushy. Add sugar to taste and bring to the boil once more. Serve with a sprinkling of chopped parsley.

Serves 4.

Test the temperature when heating cooking oil for deep-frying by dropping a 1-cm cube of bread in the oil. If it turns golden brown within 60 seconds, the oil is the right temperature.

Egg and spinach dish

Vegetable macaroni

Curried pumpkin

Vegetable pie

This pie is delicious served as a light meal with a salad. Serve with mustard or tomato sauce. Tersia Barnard of Krugersdorp serves the pie whenever they have a braai.

4 rashers bacon
1 onion, finely chopped
2 stalks celery, sliced into rings
2 leeks, sliced into rings
½ green pepper, seeded and diced
30 ml butter or margarine (optional)
2 carrots, scraped and grated
2 courgettes, rinsed and grated
1 can (410 g) whole-kernel corn, drained
100 g (250 ml) Cheddar cheese, grated
75 g (160 ml) self-raising flour
3 ml salt
1 ml paprika
1 ml thyme
4 extra-large eggs, beaten

Preheat the oven to 180 °C (350 °F). Spray a round, fairly shallow 24 x 5-cm cake tin with non-stick spray and line the base with wax paper.

Fry the bacon till crisp and chop finely. Sauté the onion, celery, leek and green pepper in the bacon fat till soft. Add the butter, if necessary. Add the remaining vegetables and stir-fry for another few minutes.

Remove from the heat and turn into the prepared cake tin.

Combine the cheese with the self-raising flour and the seasonings. Add the beaten eggs and mix well with a wire beater. Pour over the vegetables in the pan, mix lightly and bake for 35-40 minutes uncovered or till done and set.

Serves 6-8.

Vegetable pie

Potatoes and spinach

Potatoes and spinach

Spinach is very versatile and is packed with iron and calcium. Mrs Petro Papenfus says even fussy eaters who don't like spinach will be back for seconds.

3 potatoes, peeled and sliced
1 onion, sliced
oil
1 bunch (300 g) spinach (hard stems removed), shredded
salt and black pepper
1 packet (40 g) instant cheese sauce
1 packet (40 g) instant mushroom sauce
Cheddar cheese for sprinkling on top

Preheat the oven to 180 °C (350 °F). Grease an ovenproof dish with margarine.

Boil the potatoes in salted water till soft. Drain.

Sauté the onion in a little oil till soft. Add the spinach and stir-fry till the spinach is just soft. Season the mixture with salt and black pepper.

Arrange layers of potato and spinach in the dish, ending with a layer of potato. Prepare the sauces according to the instructions on the packets and pour over the ingredients in the dish. Sprinkle with a little Cheddar cheese and bake till heated through, about 30 minutes.

Serves 4.

Cook overripe tomatoes to form a purée. Bottle or freeze for later use.

Canned vegetable liquid makes a delicious, nourishing drink if blended with tomato juice. Alternatively, use it in soups, stews or casseroles.

When squeezing out oranges and lemons, reserve the squeezed out halves. Grate the zest and use for meat dishes, desserts or cake icings. Orange and lemon rind freezes well and is also much easier to grate when frozen.

Ginger dumplings

Puddings and sweets

Ginger dumplings

Serve this hot pudding with ice cream. This pudding is quick to prepare and very economical.

She always makes double the recipe because everyone comes back for seconds, writes Mrs Corrie Haasbroek of Rustenburg. The dumplings and syrup are made on top of the stove.

525 ml water
150 g (190 ml) sugar
1 ml salt
5 ml ground ginger
120 g (125 ml) butter or margarine
160 g (125 ml) smooth apricot jam
10 ml bicarbonate of soda
180 g (375 ml) cake flour
1 ml salt

In a large saucepan, heat the water, sugar, salt and ginger together on top of the stove. Stir continuously till all the sugar has dissolved, then bring the mixture to the boil.

Melt the butter in another saucepan and add the jam and bicarbonate of soda. Mix well. Add the cake flour and salt and stir till the dough no longer sticks to the sides of the saucepan. Drop teaspoonfuls of the dough into the boiling syrup. Cover the saucepan and simmer the dumplings for about 10 minutes till done.

Serve with custard, cream or ice cream.

Serves 6-8.

Sago dumplings

Sago dumplings

These dumplings are beautifully light. Mrs Martie Luies of Newcastle serves them with a cinnamon sauce or simply sprinkles cinnamon sugar over each layer of dumplings.

SAUCE
30 ml butter or margarine
5 ml cinnamon
200 g (250 ml) sugar
500 ml water
10 ml cornflour, blended with a little water

DUMPLINGS
50 ml sago
1 litre milk
pinch salt
3 eggs, separated
50 ml cornflour

Mix all the ingredients for the sauce in a large saucepan. Heat while stirring continuously and bring to the boil. Simmer till the sauce thickens slightly. Pour into a bowl and keep warm.

Prepare the dumplings: Soak the sago in a little water for about 10 minutes. Drain. Set about 15 ml milk aside and add the sago to the remaining milk. Add the salt and heat till the sago is cooked and transparent. Stir every now and then.

Beat the egg yolks lightly. Add the cornflour and 15 ml milk and mix well. Stir a little of the sago mixture into the egg mixture before adding everything to the remaining sago mixture. Simmer slowly for 5 minutes, stirring frequently.

Beat the egg whites till stiff and fold into the mixture. Drop tablespoonfuls of the mixture into the syrup and serve.

Serves 4-6.

Marmalade rice pudding

Marmalade rice pudding

Use leftover rice to make this delicious pudding. Vary the jam according to taste or what you have available. This recipe was sent in by Miss Anita Vivier of Pretoria.

75 ml marmalade
25 ml water
50 ml chopped mixed nuts
90 g (150 ml) sultanas, soaked in 100 ml sherry
600 g cooked rice
250 ml custard

Turn on the oven grill. Spray 1 large ovenproof dish or 4 small ones with non-stick spray.

Mix the marmalade, water, nuts and soaked sultanas. Heat slowly till the marmalade has just melted.

Place the rice in the prepared dish. Spoon the custard on top, pour over the marmalade mixture and grill for 2-3 minutes.

Serve immediately.

Serves 4.

Rusk crumb pudding

Rusk crumbs, potato and carrot are used to make this quick and very economical pudding, writes Miss Anita Vivier of Pretoria. The pudding makes its own delicious sauce. Serve with ice cream or custard.

80 g (250 ml) rusk crumbs
5 ml bicarbonate of soda
pinch salt
140 g (180 ml) white sugar
125 ml sultanas
250 ml grated potato
250 ml grated carrot
250 ml water
30 ml melted butter or margarine
grated rind of 1 lemon

Preheat the oven to 180 °C (350 °F). Spray a medium-sized ovenproof dish with non-stick spray.

Combine the rusk crumbs, bicarbonate of soda, salt, sugar and sultanas. Add the potato and carrot and mix. Add the water, butter and lemon rind and mix well. Turn the mixture into the prepared dish and bake for 30 minutes or till done and golden brown.

Serve with custard or ice cream.

Serves 4-6.

Cup pudding

This pudding is made in 2 cups in the microwave oven and only takes 2 minutes from start to finish, writes Clair Williams of Bloemfontein.

80 ml cake flour
2 ml baking powder
30 ml sugar
25 g butter or margarine
30 ml milk
1 egg
30 ml golden syrup or jam

Grease 2 large cups well with margarine or butter.

Sift together the dry ingredients. Melt the butter for about 1 minute in the microwave oven and add the milk and egg. Mix well and add to the dry ingredients. Mix till smooth.

Spoon 15 ml syrup into each greased cup, followed by half the batter. Cover loosely with plastic wrap and microwave for 2 minutes on 100% power. Leave for about 5 minutes before turning out onto 2 side plates.

Serve with custard, if preferred.

Serves 2.

Rusk crumb pudding

Cup pudding

Coconut bread pudding

Mrs Hannatjie du Preez of Magalieskruin collects recipes and would like to share this easy pudding recipe with us.

4 slices white bread (crusts removed), cut into pieces
375 ml hot milk
80 g (250 ml) coconut
3 eggs
300 g (375 ml) sugar
5 ml vanilla essence

Preheat the oven to 180 °C (350 °F). Grease a 1,5-litre ovenproof dish with butter or margarine.

Soak the bread in the milk for about 20 minutes and mix in the coconut. Whisk the eggs, sugar and vanilla essence together and pour over the bread mixture. Mix and pour into the prepared dish. Bake for about 25-30 minutes or till set. Serve with custard.

Serves 4-6.

Coconut bread pudding

Date loaf

Use this recipe, sent in by Mrs Annatjie Kriel of Kimberley, to make a date loaf, gingerbread or peanut loaf.

150 g dates, finely chopped
250 ml boiling water
5 ml bicarbonate of soda
60 ml oil
100 g (125 ml) sugar
100 ml golden syrup
2 extra-large eggs, whisked
300 g (625 ml) cake flour
5 ml baking powder
5 ml ground cinnamon
3 ml salt

Date loaf

Preheat the oven to 180 °C (350 °F). Spray a 23 x 13 x 7-cm loaf tin with non-stick spray.

Mix the dates, boiling water and bicarbonate of soda together and cool slightly. Add the oil, sugar and golden syrup, blending well. Cool completely before adding the whisked eggs. Mix well.

Sift the remaining ingredients together in a large mixing bowl. Make a hollow in the centre and add the date mixture. Mix thoroughly. Turn into the prepared loaf tin and bake for about 1 hour or till a testing skewer comes out clean when inserted into the centre of the loaf. Cool slightly before turning out onto a wire rack to cool completely.

Serve with butter.

Makes a medium-sized loaf.

VARIATIONS

• *For gingerbread:* Omit the dates. Substitute 15 ml ground ginger for the ground cinnamon and proceed as for the date loaf.

• *For a peanut loaf:* Omit the dates and add 125 ml chopped peanuts to the dry ingredients. Proceed as for the date loaf.

Quick lamingtons

It's always nice to end a meal with something sweet. These lamingtons are quick and inexpensive to make. Mrs Charlie Fourie of Swellendam sent us a number of ideas on how to use a ready-made sponge cake.

1 (300 g) large, round sponge cake
400 g (500 ml) sugar

125 ml water
20 ml cocoa
1 packet (200 g) coconut

Cut the cake into 3-cm cubes, reserving any leftover cake (see hint underneath).

Place all the syrup ingredients in a saucepan and heat slowly. Stir constantly till all the sugar has dissolved. Bring to the boil and simmer for 5 minutes.

Dip each cake cube in the hot syrup and roll in the coconut. If the syrup becomes too thick, slowly heat it once more.

Makes about 42 lamingtons.

HINT

• Make a delicious surprise trifle with the leftover cake. Dot pieces of the leftover cake with apricot jam and sprinkle with port or sherry, if preferred. Arrange in a dish. Pour 1 can (410 g) fruit coctail, including the syrup, over the cake. Prepare a custard with powdered milk and water and pour over. Prepare some red or green jelly and cut into pieces when set. Sprinkle the jelly over the trifle when the custard has cooled. (If preferred, add a few chopped nuts, which will increase the cost of the trifle.)

Quick lamingtons

Uncooked fudge

Uncooked fudge

Mr J J Greyling of Molteno, uses biscuit crumbs to make this sweet treat. We used Marie biscuits.

3 packets (200 g each) Marie biscuits, crushed
1 packet (500 ml) icing sugar, sifted
500 g margarine, melted
1 can (380 g) caramel condensed milk, beaten till smooth
10 ml vanilla essence
icing sugar (optional)

Spray a 27 x 39-cm baking tray with non-stick spray.

Combine the Marie biscuits and icing sugar in a mixing bowl.

Beat the margarine, caramel condensed milk and vanilla essence together till well blended. Add small quantities to the dry ingredients at a time, mixing well after each addition. Press into the baking tray and place in the fridge to harden. (Chill overnight for the best results.) Cut into squares and store in an airtight container in the fridge. Decorate with sifted icing sugar.

Makes about 60 squares.

Crustless milk tarts are prepared in a jiffy with a basic ready mix

Handy ready mixes

Ready mix for milk tart

Wonderful, is how Mrs Grace Barret of Montagu describes this instant recipe for a crustless milk tart. She was given the recipe by her friend Rykie. This ready mix is sufficient for about 13 milk tarts. The mixture must be stored in the fridge.

READY MIX
1 kg self-raising flour
1 packet (500 g) cornflour
800 g full-cream milk powder
1 kg sugar
15 ml salt
250 g margarine, grated

Mix all the dry ingredients together in a large mixing bowl. Add the margarine and rub in with your fingertips till the mixture resembles breadcrumbs. Spoon into airtight containers and store in the fridge.

Makes 20 x 250 ml ready mix.

READY MIX MILK TART

375 ml ready mix
750 ml hot water
3 extra-large eggs, separated
few drops almond essence
3 pieces stick cinnamon
cinnamon sugar for sprinkling on top

Preheat the oven to 190 °C (375 °F). Spray a 24-cm ovenproof pie dish with non-stick spray.

Add the hot water to the ready mix and mix well till all the lumps have disappeared.

Add the egg yolks, a few drops almond essence and the stick cinnamon. Heat over medium heat till the mixture comes to the boil and thickens. Stir continuously. Remove from the heat, cool slightly and remove the stick cinnamon.

Whisk the egg whites till soft peaks are formed and fold into the mixture. Pour into the prepared pie dish and bake for about 25 minutes or till the tart is done and pale brown on top. (The tart is done once the mixture has set. The mixture does, however, become even firmer as it cools and will also collapse slightly in the centre.)

Sprinkle with cinnamon sugar.

Makes a medium-sized tart.

Ready mix for scones

Freshly baked scones are delicious breakfast or tea-time treats. With this ready mix you can make four different kinds of scones in a jiffy and serve them fresh from the oven. Store the ready mix in airtight containers in the fridge and use the mixture within two weeks.

BASIC READY MIX

1,2 kg (9 x 250 ml) cake flour
225 ml low-fat milk powder
50 ml baking powder
10 ml salt
275 g butter, cut into small pieces

Sift together all the dry ingredients in a large mixing bowl. Add the pieces of butter and rub in with your fingertips till the mixture resembles mealie meal. Spoon into airtight containers and store in the fridge.

Makes 6 batches of scones of about 7 scones each.

BASIC SCONES

410 ml ready mix
125 ml iced water

Preheat the oven to 220 °C (425 °F). Spray a baking tray with non-stick spray.

Using a knife, mix the water into the ready mix till just blended. Roll out on a floured surface till 2 cm thick. Cut out circles or any other shape about 6-7 cm in diameter. Arrange at 2-cm intervals on the baking tray and brush with a little milk. Bake for 12-15 minutes or till the scones are nice and brown on top.

Serve hot with butter, honey, cheese or jam.

Makes 7-8 scones.

SWEET SCONES

410 ml ready mix
75 g (125 ml) currants
15 ml sugar
125 ml iced water

Mix the ready mix with the currants and sugar in a mixing bowl and add the water. Proceed as described in the basic scone recipe.

Makes 8 scones.

CHEESE SCONES

410 ml ready mix
50 g (125 ml) grated Cheddar cheese
1 ml cayenne pepper
125 ml iced water

Combine the ready mix with the cheese and cayenne pepper. Add the water and proceed as described in the basic scone recipe.

Makes 8 scones.

HERB SCONES

410 ml ready mix
60 ml freshly chopped herbs like parsley, dill and basil
125 ml iced water

Combine the ready mix and chopped herbs in the mixing bowl and add the water. Proceed as described in the basic scone recipe.

Makes 8 scones.

Make delicious scones with a basic ready mix

Ready mix for mealie bread

Mealie bread dough makes a delicious topping for vegetables, mince or leftover meat. Alternatively, use the ready mix to bake a mealie loaf and serve with butter, cheese, jam or honey.

Ready mix
280 g (500 ml) mealie meal
280 g (500 ml) cake flour
90 ml white sugar
25 ml baking powder
5 ml salt

Place all the ingredients in a bowl and mix well. Spoon into clean, dry containers and store in a cool place for up to 2 months.

Mealie loaf
560 ml ready mix
250 ml milk
60 ml oil
2 eggs

Preheat the oven to 200 °C (400 °F). Grease a 22 x 12 x 7-cm loaf tin with margarine.

Place the ready mix in a large bowl and make a hollow in the centre. Whisk the milk, oil and eggs together and pour into the hollow. Stir till just blended – the mixture must still be slightly lumpy.

Turn the dough into the prepared loaf tin and spread evenly. Bake uncovered for 20-25 minutes or till the top has browned slightly and a testing skewer comes out clean when inserted into the centre of the loaf.

Mealie cheese loaf
500 ml ready mix
1-2 ml cayenne pepper
250 ml milk
60 ml oil
1 egg, whisked
250 ml grated Cheddar cheese

Preheat the oven to 200 °C (400 °F). Grease a 22 x 12 x 7-cm loaf tin with margarine.

Place the ready mix in a bowl and add the cayenne pepper. Mix and make a slight hollow in the centre. Blend the milk, oil and egg and pour into the hollow. Add 125 ml grated Cheddar cheese and mix lightly till just blended. Pour into the prepared loaf tin and spread evenly. Bake for 20 minutes. Sprinkle the remaining Cheddar cheese on top and bake for 5-10 minutes.

Ready mix for white sauce

A white sauce can transform many ordinary dishes into something special. Pour it over cabbage or other vegetables of your choice and you'll have everyone coming back for seconds. Use a white sauce to bind meat, vegetables, rice or noodles for a quick meal in a dish. White sauce is also the basis for fancy soufflés and roulades.

Make this ready mix with skimmed milk powder and store in an airtight container to have on hand whenever you have to make a white sauce in a hurry.

Ready mix
1 packet (100 g) skimmed milk powder
5 ml salt
2 ml pepper
70 g (125 ml) cake flour
90 g (100 ml) butter or margarine, cut into small pieces

Sift the dry ingredients together. Using your fingertips, rub in the butter till the mixture resembles fine breadcrumbs. Store in an airtight container in the fridge for up to 1 month.

Makes 1 litre white sauce.

Basic white sauce
125 ml ready mix
250 ml water

Blend the ready mix and water in a saucepan. Heat slowly till the mixture comes to the boil and thickens. Stir continuously.

Microwave oven hint
- Place all the ingredients in a suitable container, mix well and microwave for 4 minutes on 100% power. Stir at 1-minute intervals.

Variations
- To make a thick white sauce, reduce the water to 200 ml.
- *Cheese sauce:* Add 100-200 g (250-500 ml) grated Cheddar cheese, 5 ml prepared mustard and a pinch of cayenne peper to the basic white sauce.
- *Tomato sauce:* Heat 2-3 onion rings along with the basic white sauce. Remove the onion and add 25-30 ml tomato sauce to the mixture.
- *Parsley sauce:* Add 25 ml finely chopped parsley after removing the basic white sauce from the heat.
- *Mushroom sauce:* Drain a small can of mushrooms (285 g) and add to the basic white sauce. Alternatively, slice one packet (250 g) fresh mushrooms, stir-fry till pale brown and add to the basic white sauce.

Index

Asparagus and chicken casserole 36

Bacon sandwiches 58
Baked beans with eggs 51
Baked beans with spaghetti 38
Baked fish in mustard sauce 12
Baked potatoes 68
Basic scones 77
Basic white sauce 78
Bean(s)
  and cabbage curry 63
  and meatballs 25
  and potato patties 60
  cheesy 54
Beef
  shin casserole 17
  stew 18
  stew, hearty 17
Beer stew 18
Bobotie
  chicken 37
  lentil 54
  mock 46
  samp (1) 21
  samp (2) 21
Bread
  ginger- 74
  mealie, ready mix for 78
  pan, with soya mince 57
  see also loaf
Bread and coconut pudding 74
Bread stir-fry 55
Bully beef
  and bean scone wheels 30
  and cabbage 62
  and macaroni 44
  crumble 30
  loaf 28
  pie 29
  surprise 29
  with spaghetti 40
Burgers, mealie meal 55

Cabbage
  and bean curry 63
  and bully beef 62
  and chicken with spaghetti 41
  lasagne 64
  stir-fry with bacon 62
  stir-fry with chicken 65
  stir-fry with Russians 64
  with eggs, curried 63
  with mince 64
  with salami 62
Canned potjie 16
Cheese
  loaf, mealie 78
  potato pie 66
  scones 77
Cheesy beans 54
Chicken
  and cabbage with spaghetti 41
  and sweet potato potjie 34
  bobotie 37
  casserole, asparagus and 36
  casserole with chutney 36
  delicious 35
  leftover, with herb crust 36
  paella 46
  stew 35
  with spaghetti 41
Chicken liver(s)
  and pineapple and spaghetti 39
  delight 33
  tomato 32
  with potato 32
Coconut bread pudding 74
Cottage pie with sausage 28
Creamy kidneys 31
Creamy tomato sauce spaghetti 42
Crumb topping, mince pie with 19
Crust
Cheddar crumb, leftover meat with 26
  delicious pie, shank with 15
  herb, leftover chicken with 36
  herb, sausage with 28
Cup pudding 73
Curried
  cabbage with eggs 63
  eggs and oven-baked rice 53
  fish pie 13
  mince, dumplings and 20
  potatoes 67
  pumpkin 69
Curry
  and cabbage omelette 51
  bake 20
  bean and cabbage 63
  fish 13
  red lentil 54

Date loaf 74
Delicious chicken 35
Dried beans, how to cook 67
Dumplings
  and curried mince 20
  ginger 71
  sago 72

Egg(s)
  and bacon with spaghetti (1) 40
  and bacon with spaghetti (2) 40
  and macaroni, special 52
  and rice 49
  and rice bake 50
  and spinach dish 69
  curried, and oven-baked rice 53
  in a blanket 57
  in tomato sauce 52
  with baked beans 51

Fish
  baked, in mustard sauce 12
  curry 13
  dish 7
  parcels 13
  pie, curried 13
  see also haddock, hake, pilchard(s), tuna
Fried pilchards 7
Fudge, uncooked 75

Garlic rolls 59
Ginger dumplings 71
Gingerbread 74

Haddock
  bake 8
  dish, Malay 10
  surprise 9
  with sweetcorn 9
Hake
  with rice topping 12
  with tomato 12
Hearty beef stew 17
Herb scones 77

Instant supper 23

Kidneys, creamy 31

Lamb shank in tin foil 15
Lamingtons, quick 74
Lasagne, cabbage 64
Leftover chicken with herb crust 36
Leftover meat
  rolled in scone dough 26
  with Cheddar crumb crust 26
Leftover potato pie 66
Lentil
  bobotie 54
  curry, red 54
  macaroni 43
Liver pie 32
Loaf
  bully beef 28
  date 74
  mealie 78
  mealie cheese 78
  mince meat 24
  peanut 74
  see also bread

Macaroni
  and bully beef 44
  and eggs, special 52
  lentil 43
  tuna 10
  vegetable 69
  with meatballs 43
  with pilchards in tomato sauce 6
  with sausage and potato 43
Malay haddock dish 10
Marmalade rice pudding 73
Mealie
  bread, ready mix for 78
  cheese loaf 78
  loaf 78
Mealie meal and mince casserole 22
Mealie meal bites 60
Mealie meal burgers 55
Meat
  buying hints for 33
  toppings for stews, mince or leftover meat 23
  see also leftover meat, stew(s)

.tballs
- and beans 25
- with apple sauce 25
- with macaroni 43

Milk tart, ready mix for 76
Mince
- and rice, savoury 22
- casserole, mealie meal and 22
- curried, dumplings and 20
- curry bake 20
- instant supper 23
- meat loaf 24
- pie with crumb topping 19
- surprise 23
- with putu 22
- *see also* bobotie

Mock bobotie 46

Noodles with tuna 44

Omelette
- curry and cabbage 51
- pan 52

Oven-baked rice and curried eggs 53

Paella
- chicken 46
- poor man's 45
- tuna 11

Pan bread with soya mince 57
Pan omelette 52
Pap and wors 27
Pasta
- with sour cream sauce 42
- *see also* macaroni, noodles, spaghetti

Patties
- bean and potato 60
- vegetable 61

Peanut loaf 74
Pie
- bully beef 29
- cottage, with sausage 28
- curried fish 13
- leftover potato 66
- liver 32
- mince, with crumb topping 19
- pilchard 8
- potato cheese 66
- tuna 11
- vegetable 70

Pilchard(s)
- pie 8
- fried 7
- in tomato sauce, macaroni with 6
- with yellow rice 7

Pizza bites 59
Poor man's paella 45
Pork with spaghetti 39
Potato(es)
- and bean patties 60
- and sausage supper dish 66
- and spinach 70
- baked 68
- cheese pie 66
- curried 67
- dish 68
- pan-fry 54
- pie, leftover 66

Potjie
- canned 16
- chicken and sweet potato 34

Puddings
- coconut bread 74
- cup 73
- ginger dumplings 71
- marmalade rice 73
- rusk crumb 73
- sago dumplings 72

Pumpkin, curried 69
Putu with mince 22

Quick lamingtons 74

Ready mix
- for mealie bread 78
- for milk tart 76
- for scones 77
- for white sauce 78

Ready mix milk tart 77
Red lentil curry 54
Rice
- and egg bake 50
- and eggs 49
- and marmalade pudding 73
- dish 49
- surprise 47
- with Vienna sausages 47

Risotto, Russian 48
Rolls, garlic 59
Rusk crumb pudding 73
Russian risotto 48

Sago dumplings 72
Samp
- and beans with shank 16
- and tomato dish 53
- bobotie (1) 21
- bobotie (2) 21

Sandwich(es)
- bake 58
- bacon 58

Sausage(s)
- and potato supper dish 66
- and potato with macaroni 43
- with cottage pie 28
- with herb crust 28
- wors and pap 27

Savoury mince and rice 22
Scone(s)
- basic 77
- cheese 77
- dough, leftover meat rolled in 26
- herb 77
- ready mix for 77
- sweet 77
- wheels, bully beef and bean 30

Shank
- casserole 14
- lamb, in tin foil 15
- with beans and samp 16
- with delicious pie crust 15

Sour cream sauce with pasta 42
Spaghetti
- chicken with 41
- creamy tomato sauce 42
- with baked beans 38
- with bully beef 40
- with cabbage and chicken 41
- with chicken livers and pineapple 39
- with egg and bacon (1) 40
- with egg and bacon (2) 40
- with pork 39
- with spinach 42

Special macaroni and eggs 52
Spinach
- and egg dish 69
- and potatoes 70
- with spaghetti 42

Stew(s) 14-19
- beef 18
- beef, hearty 17
- beer 18
- chicken 35

Stir-fry
- bread 55
- cabbage, with bacon 62
- cabbage, with chicken 65
- cabbage, with Russians 64

Sweet potato and chicken potjie 34
Sweet scones 77

Tomato
- and samp dish 53
- chicken livers 32
- sauce spaghetti, creamy 42

Tuna
- bake 10
- budget beater 11
- macaroni 10
- paella 11
- pie 11
- snack 56
- with noodles 44

Uncooked fudge 75

Vegetable(s)
- baked potatoes 68
- bean and cabbage curry 63
- cabbage and bully beef 62
- cabbage lasagne 64
- cabbage stir-fry with bacon 62
- cabbage stir-fry with chicken 65
- cabbage stir-fry with Russians 64
- cabbage with mince 64
- cabbage with salami 62
- curried cabbage with eggs 63
- curried potatoes 67
- curried pumpkin 69
- egg and spinach dish 69
- leftover potato pie 66
- macaroni 69
- patties 61
- pie 70
- potato cheese pie 66
- potato dish 68
- potatoes and spinach 70
- sausage and potato supper dish 66
- West-End hit 65

Vienna sausages with rice 47

West-End hit 65
White sauce
- basic 78
- ready mix for 78

Wors and pap 27